WRITING WITH THE MASTERS
FROM INTERESTS AND ABILITIES

by

Janice Neuleib

Ruth Fennick

Elaine Dion

illustrated by Dianne Ellis

Acknowledgements

The authors wish to thank archivists, librarians, teachers, and, particularly, the master authors, for their assistance and their generosity. Special thanks to family and friends for their continued interest and support.

Excerpts and manuscripts from *Voices of the River: Adventures on the Delaware* reprinted courtesy of Jan Cheripko and Boyds Mills Press.

Steinbeck photograph reproduced courtsey of the Steinbeck Archives of the Salinas Public Library, Salinas, California.

INTRODUCTION

Writing With the Masters is a series of books that offers a unique opportunity for teachers to integrate the teaching of literature and writing. These books use successful composing strategies of published authors as springboards for students' own writing. Activities providing access to the writing processes of authors enable students to trace the metamorphosis of an idea through several composing stages. Students explore the sources of a writer's ideas and the dynamics of drafting in activities using the author's additions, deletions, and rearrangements of texts in progress. In the classroom that utilizes these activities, students think, discuss, and debate composing choices. They then become active learners able to write using their own composing strategies.

From Interests and Abilities, the third book in the series, emphasizes students' unique interests and talents in writing. The activities presented have been designed with the understanding that each student has individual learning skills. One student may prefer sports, another music, another drawing, and another science or math, but each can use these talents when writing. Manuscripts and related materials of noted writers reveal a wide variety of catalysts for writing. By looking at the works of their favorite writers and the creative processes of these writers, students can discover their own strengths for writing. For example, students whose interests lie mainly in art or music can find writers who relied on art or music to help them tell their stories. Students more attracted to sports or science can find writers who drew upon their athletic or scientific interests and skills to write their stories. This book features student activities that connect reading and writing with sports, song, art, and science.

Chapter One, *Writing From Interests and Abilities,* provides a historical overview of different types of sign systems and suggests possible ways of incorporating these systems in the English/language arts curriculum to provide rich experiences for all types of learners. Student activities begin in the second chapter, *Getting to Know Your Interests and Abilities*. This chapter encourages students to see themselves as skillful meaning-makers, not only in reading and writing but also in other ways. Chapters three through six focus on various types of skills that enhance reading and writing abilities.

The lessons follow a set format. Each unit begins with *Notes to the Teacher*, designating the composing strategies highlighted and providing background information. Student activities begin with the *Getting to Know* sections, which focus on understanding and interpreting the featured literary work. In the *Writing About* sections, students respond to their reading of that work in various types of writing. *Writing With* sections encourage students to write their own texts, incorporating some of the authors' composing strategies.

Seeing master writers at work can help both teachers and students learn to tap their unique gifts to generate ideas and to enjoy making choices while writing and revising. The activities engage students in lively group discussions and give them freedom to write creatively. This integrated approach to the teaching of literature and composition encourages critical thinking and student initiative in learning.

1

WRITING FROM INTERESTS AND ABILITIES

Language arts teachers from kindergarten through college have all had the experience of sitting next to someone on a bus or plane and being asked, "What do you do?" When the answer to the question is "I teach English" or "I teach language arts," the questioning passenger often says, "I was never good at that" or "I'll have to watch my grammar." Most of us have never had anyone respond, "Oh, I loved drawing pictures to illustrate my book reports in fifth grade" or "When I was little, I liked to sing the Pooh songs along with my father when he read to me." Most teachers find that the general public perceives writing as putting symbols on paper or computer, not as a complex and exciting system of signs, symbols, and ideas. For most people, writing instruction all too often invokes the image of the red pen run over pages of hapless and hopeless student texts. Most people forget that writing and reading are the manipulation of many kinds of textual clues, often including pictures, word problems, and poetic musical rhythms. Writers who want to write really wonderful stories must learn to use all of these systems.

- Ray Bradbury emphasized the importance of appealing to all of the reader's senses. Nose, eye, ear, tongue, and hand, he claimed, need to be "assaulted" if the reader is going to believe and thereby participate in the story or poem.

Historical Connections Among Sign Systems

Picture Writing

Historically, everywhere in the world writing began with pictures. The earliest cave drawings are still visible in caves in modern Europe. These drawings began as pictures of actions, but in time, the pictures became individual symbols for those actions and for sounds as a part of the actions. Thus, ancient languages—for example, Old Norse with its runes, ancient Chinese with its pictographs, and Native American signs—are symbol systems that equate the word with the action pictured. Even today, students play games that use picture symbols for words, often as part of units on Native Americans.

Runes were ancient letters in a sign system. These letters themselves were meaningful. The letters, having derived from pictures, supposedly carried the power of their original picture sources. Poems or riddles written in runic characters became a kind of trickster language that carried the meaning of the picture along through the signs themselves. To this day, Finnish poems are called "runes." Note the shapes of the runes below. Some look like letters, and some look like drawings.

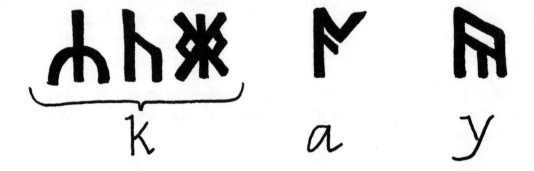

Stories in Song

As time passed, Anglo-Saxon poets—called scops, bards, or minstrels—wandered throughout the countryside singing the runic poems, incorporating the drawings into songs and small skits. Later, assembled town and castle folk added dance and chanting to the singing of the poets. In Ireland and parts of modern-day France, similar poets sang to early people called Celts, who valued the power of these poems that had been set to music. To this day, the symbol of old Ireland remains a beautiful hand-carved harp which reflects the power that these ancient songs still hold for people in that country.

Even older, familiar stories about music and poetry can be found in ancient, sacred books like the Bible and in Hindu stories and tales. One familiar Biblical tale tells of King David, who played a lyre or harp and danced to celebrate victories and other great events in his kingdom. Siva, a god of great power in Hindu mythology, dances a fire dance that creates and destroys life. In British mythology, Merlin, King Arthur's magician, sings the stones at Stonehenge—the great circle of rocks in southern England—into their places. Music and dance weave inextricably through stories of battle and victory, of life and death, and of creation and destruction.

Theater and Dance

Drama and religion have often been linked throughout history. Greek plays were performed in temples, and the first medieval plays were simply Biblical tales acted out in chapels and cathedrals. Dance and theater were also connected long before the American musical became popular. The Greeks had dances and musical accompaniment connected with their plays.

Stories inevitably contain elements of action that can be translated into drama. When storytellers begin to write their stories, they naturally imagine the play that might grow from that story, as well as the music and dance that could enhance it. Fiction and poetry nearly always have musical or lyrical elements present or implied.

Sports Stories

The drama of a great sporting event hardly needs to be explained, but all sports have a story and are potential subjects for writing. Like art, music, and dance, sporting events also have origins that predate historical records. In fact, many of our most popular sports may have archetypal origins reflecting experiences of early cave dwellers—the baseball bat suggesting a stick or club and the ball a stone, and the animal hide on a football symbolizing the hunt. The Olympic games, dating at least as far back as ancient Greece, involved athletes honoring the gods in contests of jumping, footracing, discus throwing, javelin throwing, wrestling, boxing, and chariot racing. These historical sporting events are reflected in some of our most popular movies and books. Who can forget Ben Hur's chariot races or Robin Hood's skill at archery?

In fact, more people probably read about sports than about any other subject. Some of the fastest readers are baseball fans who can scan and digest a page of statistics in the twinkling of an eye, and everyone loves to tell stories of the fish that got away, the stolen base, or the spike that saved the game in the last second. Nearly every writer tells a sport story at one time or another. Ernest Hemingway's *The Old Man and the Sea* may be one of the most famous, although almost all of Hemingway's writings have a sport element of some kind.

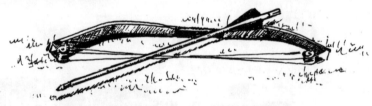

Language and Logic

Although language arts and the sciences are often thought of as distinctly different areas of study, connections between them are strong. As with sports, formal connections between these two subjects date back at least to ancient Greece where rhetoric developed as a scientific method of inquiry emphasizing reason and logic. It was Aristotle who first catalogued the means by which rhetoricians—like modern scientists—could most effectively select their evidence and argue their cases, usually in courts and legislative bodies. For rhetoric to be persuasive, however, it needed more than facts. It also had to have emotional appeals that often were more effective when set in poetic language. As rhetoric evolved, it took on various focuses, including style and delivery. Today, rhetoric draws on many areas of inquiry, including psychology, sociology, philosophy, and all of the English language arts, including literature.

Connections between story writing and science as a subject, rather than a method of inquiry, are even more apparent in our society today. Popular culture abounds in stories focusing on everything from prehistoric dinosaurs to intergalactic travel, reflecting our need to explain the inexplicable. Rarely does a movie season pass without a blockbuster about some exotic biological mutation threatening human existence. Like ancient cultures, we create new myths and legends to explain natural phenomena and to express our fears of the unknown.

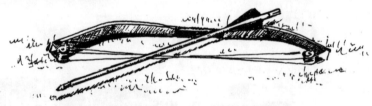

Multiple Intelligences in the Classroom

Individual Differences

Psychologist Robert Sternberg has identified three kinds of intellectual ability: analytical, creative, and practical. The analytical student scores well on standardized tests and earns high marks in school. The creative student is less remarkable on standard tests but excels in originality. The practical student is a survivor, able to adapt to new situations with relative ease.

Howard Gardner looks at individual differences a little differently and has identified seven types of intelligence: linguistic, musical, logical-mathematical, spatial, bodily-kinesthetic, intrapersonal, and interpersonal. Other researchers have developed yet other classifications, but what comes through in all of these studies is that individuals learn in uniquely different ways. Most people have some ability in a variety of learning modes, but they usually shine in only a few. These abilities reflect not only individual preferences and interests but also different creative processes and different ways of making meaning.

The difficulty for the classroom teacher is that learning preferences in a single class will cover the whole range of abilities. Furthermore, the majority of the students may not share the teacher's learning strengths—one of which will most certainly be linguistic ability. Although linguistic and mathematical abilities are privileged in our culture, they are not as highly prized in some other cultures, where musical, spatial, or kinesthetic abilities may be more valued. With the increasingly diverse cultural makeup of classrooms, the whole range of competencies takes on greater significance. Equally important, studies of connections between physical movement and thinking, particularly the influence of hand and eye on cognitive activity, show that activities involving hand, eye, and brain activity appear to enhance learning—especially when these activities occur simultaneously.

Integrating Multiple Modes

The arts—visual, aural, and performing—are especially rich areas for developing and reinforcing linguistic skill because the processes of creating and expressing meaning are similar in many ways. In each case, the artist, musician, writer, or actor attempts to understand, clarify, and order the world in some way and, generally, to convey the ideas and emotions to others through some tangible form. Artists generate initial concepts by sketching half-formed ideas and, through multiple revisions, they arrive at the finished product. Musicians work similarly, sketching musical notes, listening to the early draft on a musical instrument, and revising until the "text" corresponds to the emerging mental concept. Even more physical kinds of performances require similar integration of body and mind. Dancers, for example, express mental concepts through meticulously choreographed and rehearsed movements.

Language arts teachers can integrate these various ways of learning by creating different types of experiences in the study of particular subject matter. For example, one student may respond to a story with his or her own narrative, another with an analytical response, another with pictures or song lyrics, and yet another with choreographed movements. When these varied responses are shared, all students learn something new about the story, about their peers, about themselves, and about different ways of learning.

Once students recognize that they have individual learning styles—learning styles that reflect strengths rather than limitations—they will be able to better recognize that some of their favorite authors share their particular learning styles. Upon this discovery, the students stand a greater chance of increasing their literacy and, at the same time, finding joy and satisfaction in it.

Kinesthetic Ability

Very often, student athletes consider literature and writing as things that more "bookish" students do. This view is unfortunately confirmed in too many popular movies showing star athletes succeeding in spite of minimal literacy skills. And too often, advocates of sports programs for at-risk students further emphasize sports as an alternative rather than an avenue to academic success. Such one-sided approaches to learning and literacy unfairly limit these students' potential. A more effective approach recognizes that all people have talents and that strengths in one area can be tapped to enhance abilities in other areas. Movement—like writing—helps an athlete demonstrate a particular skill. And like art or music, movement can be seen as a type of artistic expression. The connection is more immediately obvious in some activities than others—dance, gymnastics, swimming or diving, for example—but movement on a basketball court or baseball field requires similar grace and precision, as well as a controlling sense of purpose.

Athletes, of course, are not the only people who use their kinesthetic and tactile senses to make meaning. Anyone who has spent five minutes in a middle school is keenly aware of the immense energy and physicality of adolescent students. Rather than walking straight down a hallway, students are more likely to chart a zigzag course, good naturedly tapping one student, punching another, slapping the wall, and swinging their book bags as they make their way to class. Although some students are able to channel this energy productively in the classroom, teachers know that others simply cannot. For some students, sitting still for a fifty-minute class period is not only difficult, it is impossible.

In many cases, these students' difficulty may have less to do with academic ability or inclination than with learning style. An increasing number of research studies have shown that some students are primarily kinesthetic learners, who learn in different ways from analytic or auditory learners. Because kinesthetic learners appear to learn more globally, they have particular difficulty with instructional methods that emphasize sequential bits of information in formal skill and drill. Rather, they excel in activities that move from whole to part and, especially, in high interest, hands-on activities, such as writing on computers, drawing pictures, acting out plays, reading aloud, playing games, and writing their own stories. In fact, many famous writers have emphasized the importance of physical activity as a part of their writing processes.

Large Motor Skills

- *The Red Pony* reflects John Steinbeck's riding experiences with his own red pony, Jill, which he rode in the horse parade for the California Rodeo. In *The Red Pony*, the character Jody dreams of riding in this rodeo.

- Charles Dickens found that physical exercise helped him avoid the energy drain resulting from the intense emotional physical requirements of writing. In his notebook, he claimed that while writing one of his novels, he worked from nine o'clock until two o'clock and then walked until five in the afternoon.

- Tennessee Williams also felt that physical activity was necessary to compensate for the nervous energy created by writing. His customary practice was to swim 16 to 20 lengths in a pool every day.

- Like Dickens, Edith Wharton worked every morning, and in the afternoon, she took a long walk until time for tea.

- Ray Bradbury says that writers who want to feed their personal Muse must take long walks around the city by night and around the country by day.

- Margaret I. Roskowski enjoys both watching and participating in sports activities. She regularly watches live baseball, explores the land where she lives, and walks with her dog every day.

Small Motor Skills

Even the physical act of writing—putting symbols on paper or signing in American sign language—is an important kinesthetic and tactile activity that is experienced differently by different writers. Some famous writers feel that they must compose on typewriters or computers, whereas others need to feel the pencil in their hands gliding over the paper. Some writers do both at different times.

- Steinbeck not only needed just the right kind of pencil, but he had to have different types of pencils for different days. Depending on whether it would be what he called a "hard writing day" or a "soft writing day," he would choose pencils with hard or soft lead.

- Faulkner also wrote initially in longhand, claiming that he needed to feel the pencil in his hand and see the words emerging at the point. The second draft, he composed on the typewriter.

Orality and Musical Ability

Music

If you watch people jogging, walking, or bicycling, chances are they will be wearing headsets. If a car radio or tape player is broken, the car is likely to be considered almost unusable, unless a battery powered version is readily available.

Everyone who listens to music knows that songs are the most common stories that are "read." But even music that has no lyrics tells a story. It is not hard to imagine different themes for a piano sonata and a rock song. The strong connections between stories and music are especially apparent in movie sound tracks. Imagine an exciting chase scene and think of the music that would accompany it. Then imagine the background music for a spring romance scene. Even the most amateur musicians among us know the scores are not interchangeable. In fact, often the sound track—with the story permanently inscribed in its notes and nuances—lives on long after the film itself has gone to the back shelves in the video store.

As in ancient cultures, we continue to use music as a major mode of communication. We preserve stories through recitations, songs, and ballads, sometimes in written form but not always. Sometimes the stories recount events of times long past or attempt to explain natural phenomena. Other times, they emerge from the present culture, reflecting our customs, values, activities, and shared concerns. Some songs are sung as a way of remembering content, such as the songs young children sing to memorize the alphabet. And many songs and stories are acted out in theatrical productions.

Music can make a person feel happy, sad, excited, calm, or irritated. In fact, just as people have reading preferences—spy stories or romance novels, for example—their music tastes are often quite diverse. Some people love jazz with its unpredictable twists and turns. Others hate it, needing greater predictability. "Elevator" music is soothing to some people, while others find it unbearably boring. Music can relieve depression, providing reassurance that people care, that people are fundamentally good, that world peace may be possible. Classical music inspires some people to respond this way. On the other hand, music can also increase depression. Country and western songs about infidelity, alcoholism, poverty, and the accompanying heartbreak are possible examples. In fact, research shows that this sensitivity and response to sound is an innate feature of all living creatures. Infants and even animals respond to the sounds of the voices around them. They recognize rhythms and tonal distinctions even when they do not understand the words. They recognize and respond favorably to harmony. Similarly, they recognize discord and respond accordingly in apprehension.

Music may also make a person's brain work better. Recent studies show that music lessons, and even listening to music, can improve spatial reasoning. Other research has shown that music therapy can help people with brain injuries.

As with kinesthetic ability, many noted writers use their musical interests and inclinations in their writing.

- Paul Fleischman claims that words are musical, something he discovered when he listened to languages he did not understand. He is an avid music listener and likes even more to play music. This musical interest, he says, led directly to the writing of some poems and later to several books.

- Harriet Tubman often used music to express her feelings about slavery and her desire to be free.

- One of Edgar Allan Poe's most famous poems was originally titled, "The Bells: A Song."

- Maya Angelou is a singer, dancer, conductor, and song writer. She writes song lyrics for her own songs, as well as for other singers. Following a tragic experience that left her mute for six years, she developed great pleasure in the sounds of the human voice, sounds that she reproduces in the rich cadence of her work. One of her book titles, *I Know Why the Caged Bird Sings,* reflects her interest in music.

Orality

Although much is yet to be known about thought and language connections, it is clear that articulation not only reflects thought but also generates it. Talk, because it relies on a fully engaged speaker and ideally a fully engaged listener, provides an opportunity for intense thinking.

Many famous writers report using this strategy for thinking about their work.

- John Steinbeck read his work aloud to his wife Elaine and also customarily read his manuscripts aloud into a dictating machine. He then played the recording back to hear the sound of what he had written.

- Each evening over the telephone, Edith Wharton read what she had written that morning page by page to her editor and friend Walter Berry.

- Charles Dickens also claimed to have read page proofs aloud. One of his auditors was a mysterious, unnamed woman, who, he said, gave him advice about his stories.

- Mark Twain, who found the pen sometimes inhibiting, is reported to have talked and talked until he felt he got his dialogue right.

- Tennessee Williams also claimed to talk out the lines as he wrote.

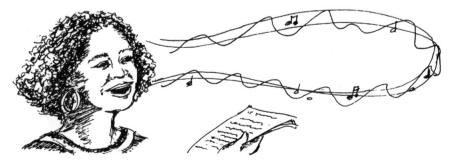

Visualization and Artistic Ability

Like early cultures which used pictures carved in stone as a way of recording historical events and passing them on to future generations, modern artisans similarly preserve elements of contemporary culture. A trip to any public park reveals pictures, messages, and initials carved into wood and stone, as though the carver, like our ancient ancestors, felt compelled literally to leave a mark in the world. Especially apparent in communities across the nation are the gang culture's highly complex symbols, or turf markings, which pictorially emblazon for themselves and others who they are.

These modern pictographs reflect the centuries-old practice of connecting writing and art. In fact, early manuscripts were often valued more for their artistic worth than for their communicative ability. Ornate calligraphy and decorative borders elaborately depicted historical events in elegant and often humorous "illuminations" of animals, floral elements, Biblical scenes, and heroic figures. Illustrations in today's story books continue this practice of complementing or "completing" the story only partly told by the words.

The creative process of art parallels the creative process in writing. Manuscripts of famous artworks show the artist creating a rough sketch and revising it through multiple drafts, much as writers do as they strive to find the meaning and then express it. In fact, Seurat's famous painting *La Grande Jatte* is reported to have been revised 57 times.

Many writers rely on images and pictures in their writing.

- C. S. Lewis claimed that in writing *The Chronicles of Narnia,* images came before the words. He started out with the image of a faun, and as he continued to write, the images continued as well. He had intended to write only one story, but the images continued and before he knew it, he had completed seven volumes. In fact, Lewis claimed that his earliest writings were picture stories that he wrote with his brother.

- E. B. White drew the neighbor's barn and a picture of a spider in its web to help him write *Charlotte's Web*.

- F. Scott Fitzgerald relied on pictures to get a clear vision for *The Great Gatsby*. He had his wife Zelda draw endless sketches until he felt he had an intimate sense of the person Gatsby.

- Edith Wharton was convinced that visualization was related in some way to genius.

- Tennessee Williams said that for him everything was visual. His text appeared to him as if it were on a lit stage.

- Ray Bradbury routinely drew pictures to help him think of ideas for his stories.

- Roald Dahl collected pictures of people for the details of the eyes, nose, mouth, and expression and used them when describing characters.

Logical Thinking: Scientific and Mathematical Ability

Of all the many artificial compartmentalizations of one discipline from another, probably no gap is greater than that between the humanities and the sciences, especially mathematics. English/language arts students can read, write, and talk about historical events, social problems, vocational interests, and even plants and animals, but the connection to mathematical concepts seems remote at best. However, when we look at how learning occurs, we see that common intellectual processes unite the disciplines. Both writers and mathematicians look closely at observable phenomena in an attempt to find patterns and, thereby, create meaning. Science and math are not just about facts and numbers any more than writing is just about proofreaders' marks. Both disciplines use accepted facts in the construction of new knowledge, and both use symbolic forms to express that knowledge. The same analytical ability that scientists use in the laboratory is useful in examining a literary work or a friend's written or oral argument.

Although some students who excel in math find linguistic study discouraging, math apprehension may be even greater in students whose strengths lie more in linguistic ability. However, just as all small children have extensive linguistic competence, everyone from an early age also has a great deal of intuitive math knowledge. Studies show that preschool children are able to solve problems using a variety of strategies that they have not been formally taught. Given simple math problems, they are able to complete a wide range of mathematical operations including addition, subtraction, multiplication, and division. These operations can be solved with the help of logic and such concrete objects as building blocks and fingers which help in the computation.

Teachers can help students tap into their intuitive knowledge in all disciplines by helping students to see what they already know, reducing the amount of time spent on drills, increasing the time spent on solving problems both individually and in groups, and encouraging investigation of problems that have personal significance. By helping students see connections rather than divisions among fields of study, teachers can use knowledge in one area to develop knowledge in another. Approaching a subject in the spirit of inquiry encourages students' natural curiosity and invites the kind of integration that is natural in the world outside the classroom. Students trained in inquiry-based learning are less likely to venerate content knowledge. Instead, they will learn to value the process of discovery in the construction of knowledge.

Many famous writers used scientific inquiry and subject matter in creating their stories.

- Mary Shelley's *Frankenstein,* which raises questions about scientists' responsibilities for their creations, resulted from speculations Shelley had with several friends about the possibilities of generating life in a laboratory.

- H. G. Wells' interest in science resulted in *The Time Machine,* which used a school essay he had written titled "The Man of the Year Million." Also important contributors to Wells' book were his reading and discussions with friends on the subject of evolution.

- Sir Arthur Conan Doyle had his famous detective Sherlock Holmes, with the help of Dr. Watson, solve all of his cases using reason and observation.

- Isaac Asimov, one of our most prolific writers, used his background as a biochemist to make scientific subjects understandable for general readers.

Writing as a Mental and Physical Process

The attention successful writers give to the environment, to their physical activities, and to the tools of their trade suggests that writing is not only a mental activity but also a physical act—an act that plays a significant role in the overall process. The role of physical exercise and ritual behavior in writing may reflect the need to maintain a measure of control in an otherwise abstract and chaotic process. Perhaps taking long walks and swimming help trigger some kind of creative mental state. Rituals, no doubt, free the mind from procedural concerns, allowing greater attention to the conceptual problems at hand.

Visual and aural activities, customarily considered typical of younger or more inexperienced writers, apparently continue in some form into maturity. Researchers studying children's writing behavior have observed that children tend to speak aloud and make visual representations as they write. This oral and visual activity, it was assumed, reflects children's need to externalize language. As children matured, researchers concluded, they were able to internalize language activity.

However, as we have seen, highly successful writers appear to rely a great deal on talking and picture-making. Rather than reflecting immaturity, these activities may actually reflect fairly sophisticated strategies for simplifying the complex demands of language. Pictures and spoken words convey messages more directly than written language. Reading words aloud, for example, eliminates an intermediate step in language processing. Because written words are actually visual images of spoken words, they need to be "translated" back into sounds before the reader can process them. This translation process occurs so rapidly that most readers are not even aware of it. Furthermore, by slowing the reading process, the writer is able to discover gaps or inconsistencies that more rapid, silent reading can easily miss.

The units in this book provide students with activities designed to encourage them to imitate strategies practiced by some of the most successful writers. Because the focus of this book is writing, each unit provides teaching suggestions to help students identify their learning preferences and to use these preferences to become better writers. The book is arranged into chapters focusing on kinesthetic, musical, artistic, and scientific/mathematical abilities. However, the activities presented in each unit in these chapters necessarily involve more than one of these types of abilities. In fact, sometimes they include all of them. Because all of the chapters feature activities for improving linguistic competence and performance, linguistic ability is not included as a separate chapter.

In the chapters, students will use writing to discover some of their unique interests and abilities. They will share scientific observations based on their exploration and investigation of the world around them. They will draw pictures, write poems, sing songs, play instruments, write narratives, play sports, give talks, and publish books from these experiences. In these and other ways, students will expand their range of abilities and make their thinking visible.

GETTING TO KNOW YOUR
INTERESTS AND ABILITIES

Writers need to know that composition can happen in many ways. Humans communicate meaning in many complex and subtle ways. This chapter helps writers to see which ways of making meaning work best for them as individual writers. The chapter begins with a general questionnaire that will help students focus on all the ways they can use writing to communicate ideas. The questionaire asks the students to choose means of communication that appeal most to them (pages 14 and 15). The students answer questions about kinesthetic, aural, visual, and quantitative ways of knowing. Students are asked to work alone and together to decide which ways of making meaning work best for them in both individual and group situations. For instance, some people may sit down and play the piano to get relaxed and ready to write, whereas others might actually write the words to a song while composing at the piano.

The idea of using music or dance or basketball as a way of composing will probably be new to students, at least until they think about the books and songs they like the most. Then the multiplicity of the ways in which people learn become obvious. As students work through these activities, they see that they have varied talents, some of which may not be tapped often enough by our visual culture. People tend to think too often in terms of reading and writing, less often of speaking and listening, and far less often of sculpting and acting out. The latter has even become a psychological term of derision. Yet for some students "acting out" may be the best route to an understanding of a problem or to the composition of a work.

For many students this kinesthetic way of learning is the most desirable. Not only does this questionnaire help students discover their best kinesthetic skill, but the activities will also help them work through those discoveries in action and words. The same is true of the musical, artistic, and quantitative questionnaires. Students discover and have a chance to reflect on the areas that please them most and to discover ways to direct their own preferences.

Using Multiple Ways of Learning

Too often ability is associated with "book learning." In fact, there are many different ways of learning and perfecting different abilities. To get a picture of yourself as a learner, answer the following questions. Place an X in the blank in front of those activities you would like to do.

1. Which of the following activities would you prefer to perform when given the school task of reviewing a book you have read or a video you have seen?

    _____ a. Write a response to or summary of the book/video.

    _____ b. Draw an illustration or take a photograph that captures the point of the story.

    _____ c. Act out a scene from the story with a group of friends.

    _____ d. Give an oral report to the class.

    _____ e. Tell your teacher about the story in private.

2. Check the activities you would choose if you had free time that had to be spent on a school activity and the freedom to choose your own activity.

    _____ a. Work on a sport for a competitive or intramural team.

    _____ b. Go to the band or choral room and work on your music.

    _____ c. Find a computer and work on a project.

    _____ d. Sit down in a quiet place to read.

    _____ e. Talk to a friend about a project.

    _____ f. Work with a teacher who had the time to meet with you.

    _____ g. Get together with a group to finish a project.

3. What is your favorite part of the school day? Number in order of preference.

_____ a. Getting together with friends before and after class

_____ b. Music classes

_____ c. Math and science classes

_____ d. Literature and writing classes (journalism, yearbook)

_____ e. Tech prep and hands-on classes

_____ f. Theater and speech classes/activities

_____ g. Athletic practice and events

_____ h. Art classes

Look back at your responses and notice how you responded to the questions. Do you prefer to be in motion doing sports or dance? Would you prefer to be playing music or working in a class with music in the background? Would you rather create an art project than write an essay or story? Would you like a math or science project to take up a larger part of your day? We all have preferences when it comes to how we learn best. Often combining two or three types of activities can be stimulating, as the example of writing to music indicates. Perform the following activity to get an even sharper picture of yourself as a learner.

4. Find out who in your class has answers similar to yours for the questions about favorite parts of the class day. Get together in groups with your fellow "learners" and perform your preference. For example, if you prefer to learn through art, make a poster indicating your preference. If you like sports, think how a game can teach you something about another subject. For example, you might talk about how a particular sport teaches about other knowledge, i.e. we may learn to overcome fears about facing strangers by learning to ride a horse, or we may learn how to divide by figuring batting averages.

On another sheet of paper, illustrate and describe your group's discussion.

Kinesthetic Ability

Place an X in the blanks which designate activities that you would like to do.

1. If you were at the gym, what kind of activity would you do?

   _____ Pick-up basketball   _____ League basketball

   _____ Running   _____ Aerobics

   _____ Weightlifting   _____ Swimming for a team

   _____ Swimming alone   _____ Racquetball

   _____ Volleyball   _____ Other (please specify)

2. Would you rather _____ dance or _____ play football?

3. Would you rather _____ play soccer or _____ ride a bicycle?

4. Would you rather _____ play rugby or _____ ride a horse?

5. Describe your favorite spectator sport. Do you watch it on TV or in person or both?

   _____

   _____

   _____

   _____

6. Describe your favorite participatory sport or athletic activity.

   _____

   _____

   _____

   _____

7. Talk with your group about a process that you can do. Each of you should describe it in as much detail as you can. For example, if you are telling how to make an ice cream soda, remember to describe how the glass should feel and what color the ice cream and liquid should be. Try to include as much tactile and other sense detail as you can. Each person in the group should describe a process.

    Now write a description of your process. Be certain not to miss any details of movement, sound, smell, or taste. Sight is usually described first, but kinesthetic learning often takes place at these other sensory levels.

    _____

    _____

    _____

    _____

    _____

    _____

    _____

    _____

8. What have you discovered about yourself as a kinesthetic learner? Do you like lively, participatory games and sports, or are you the take-a-quiet-walk-in-the-woods sort? Would you rather dance than run? Would you rather feel a bow expand in your hands than feel a table tennis ball bounce off your paddle?

    Write a paragraph here about yourself in motion. How do you like best to be in motion?

    _____

    _____

    _____

    _____

    _____

    _____

    _____

Musical Talent and Aural Learning

Most of us can remember the words to a poem better if those words are set to music and if we hear them sung. People who learn best aurally prefer to learn the way most of us like to learn lyrics. To test your aural learning, ask a friend to read a passage from one of your textbooks to you. Then read the next passage yourself. Which one do you remember better? Now try reading aloud yourself. For some people the reinforcement of both reading and hearing at the same time works best. It is important to know how visual or aural you are to know what kind of studying and learning situation works best for you.

1. If you were playing music, what kind would you listen to? Place an X next to the kind of music you enjoy.

   _____ Rock'n'Roll   _____ Quiet, semi-classical

   _____ Country   _____ Jazz

   _____ Classical   _____ Other (please specify)

2. Do you play a musical instrument or sing? What instrument? What voice do you sing?

   _____
   _____
   _____
   _____
   _____

3. Describe your experiences with musical performances or with watching others perform.

   _____
   _____
   _____
   _____
   _____

4. In your group, read aloud a passage that describes a scene or a process (putting together a bicycle or preparing a type of food, for example). Have each person write down what he or she heard after the reading. Who got the most information? Who got the least? How does learning by ear work for each of you? Do you prefer to learn this way? Discuss your responses with your group members.

5. Find a set of song lyrics that you enjoy. Write or paste them below. Compare your choice with a friend's choice. What effect does the music have on your feelings about the words to the song?

6. Nearly everyone likes to be read to; note the popularity of taped novels for long car trips. Choose a selection of short stories, poems, or musical lyrics. Take turns reading them in your group. Write down your reactions both to reading and listening. Which was more pleasant for you? Discuss your reactions with group members. Then write your reactions to the readings below. Briefly retell the story or describe the lyrics. Do you recall the reading or the listening better?

_____
_____
_____
_____
_____
_____
_____
_____
_____
_____

Artistic Talent and Pictorial Learning

Our society values visual learning and artistic expression. Television and videos (whether in the theater or at home) are a chief source of entertainment for many. Even sporting events become a kind of visual experience when translated to the screen. People also enjoy treating themselves as artistic canvases, sometimes using strange hair colors or amazing fashions. Women have always used paint to enhance their faces, and all actors, both male and female, do so on stage. Many people also turn quickly to the cartoons in the newspapers, sometimes cutting out particularly significant pictures and multiple frames to display on refrigerators, lockers, or offices. Pictures speak a thousand words.

1. Draw a picture of yourself below. You can use a stick figure or be as elaborate as you wish. Around the picture, sketch or draw in items or symbols that tell something about you. For example, someone who likes horses would draw horses or cowboy hats.

2. Join your group and compare the drawings you made. Check similarities and differences. After talking with group members, add anything to your picture that seems to enhance it.

3. Visit an art gallery (one at your school is fine) or choose a movie to attend or to watch at home on video. As you view pictures or watch the movie, list the images that affect you. Also, list anything you particularly responded to, such as humor or strong visual effects. Now consider your list and write about your responses to the visual images.

_____
_____
_____
_____
_____
_____
_____

4. Ask each person in your group to bring a portrait to school. The person bringing the picture should know something about the subject of the portrait (who it is, when it was taken, a story behind the picture if possible), but the information should be kept secret until after the activity. As each person in the group passes a portrait around, write down your reactions to each one. Make some guesses about who the person in the photograph is. Then discuss what you wrote down as individual group members and compare your reactions to the "facts" about the subject of the portrait.

5. Sculpture and architecture often go unnoticed even though they can be found everywhere. Bring to your group either a sculpture (or the picture of a sculpture) that you find interesting or symbolic, or bring in a picture of a house or building that you find unusual or meaningful. Pass around the sculptures or pictures, and write briefly about the images. Discuss your responses to each form. What kinds of architecture do you prefer? What kinds of sculpture?

_____
_____
_____
_____
_____
_____
_____
_____
_____

Science and Mathematics: Measuring the World and Finding Meaning

Scientific reasoning involves carefully noting the world around us and recording those notations. Then we must try to make some sense of what has been noted. We use this kind of reasoning every time we say, "Oh, I shouldn't eat cheeseburgers; they're filled with cholesterol and calories!" or "The grass has no dew this morning; it will rain before evening." Such comments assume many kinds of scientific and quantitative knowledge. Research tells us that animal fat may create blockages in our arteries. The weather person will also tell us that a dewless morning suggests rain, unless you happen to be in the desert.

1. Think about how you personally would like to do scientific research. Would you like to (check as many as you like):

   _____ weigh yourself daily?   _____ study child growth?

   _____ dig for dinosaurs?   _____ learn about rockets?

   _____ observe zoo animals?   _____ figure out taxes?

   _____ use a microscope/telescope?   _____ grow plants?

2. Bring to your group a report of either a recent scientific finding or a statistical study of some current event (like how many were injured in a storm or some other event). Write about what the researchers expect you to know in order to understand the study. Discuss your study with group members. What did you choose to bring and why?

3. List the kinds of "science" you can remember. Compare your list to those of others in your group. Discuss what you know about the sciences. List the ones you might consider learning more about. List the ones that do not interest you at all.

4. Watch a science program on television or read a popular science report. Describe the information for your group members and discuss which information was the most interesting or useful to each of you.

5. What careers are you considering? Make a list of possibilities. Now make a list of the scientific and mathematical knowledge you will need to be able to work in your chosen field. Compare your list with those of other students. Which careers demand the most scientific and quantitative knowledge? If possible, interview someone in your chosen field to confirm your guesses about the scientific and quantitative knowledge required for the field. Report back to your class.

KINESTHETIC ABILITY

The current focus on integrating disciplines in the schools grows out of a belief in the importance of educating the whole child. When children experience the world outside of school, knowledge is not fragmented and compartmentalized. Events occur in a context and a community that include ability and knowledge in many disciplines. Classrooms that integrate disciplines and accommodate multiple learning styles enable students to strengthen their individual abilities and develop others.

The master writers highlighted in this chapter reflect this integrated approach to learning in the merging of kinesthetic and linguistic abilities. Canoeing, hunting, and baseball are all used, both as content for writing and as catalysts for, and sometimes even the means of, artistic and symbolic expression. In *Voices of the River: Adventures on the Delaware,* for example, Jan Cheripko not only writes about a sports adventure, but he thinks in sports-related measurements, noting that the width of the river at its origins is the length of a football field.

Activities in the following units ask students to imitate the practices of these writers, participating in various kinds of sports and then writing about them. Kinesthetic learners, especially when they are reluctant writers, see from these activities that mental and physical fitness are closely related. When they also discover that some of their favorite writers are physically active learners like themselves, they begin to see their own abundant energy and natural curiosity as assets rather than limitations. They see that they too can do well in language classes, not in spite of their interest in sports, but because of it.

The first unit in this chapter, featuring Jan Cheripko's *Voices of the River: Adventures on the Delaware,* shows students how their interest in sports and love of the outdoors can help them improve their writing abilities. Cheripko and his co-author Matthew Smith took a 215-mile canoe trip on the Delaware River, recording their observations in writing and film. The result is a photo-journal capturing the thrills and dangers of the trip, as well as the historical richness and natural beauty of the land along the Delaware. Writing activities in this unit focus on Cheripko's writing process and include an early manuscript page from the book, his editor's responses, and his own comments on the writing of the book. Students are asked to imitate Cheripko's process by planning their own journey, taking notes, recording the experience in pictures, writing a preliminary draft, getting feedback from an editor, revising the draft, and publishing the adventure in their own photo-journal.

Wilson Rawls's *Where the Red Fern Grows,* a story about hunting, is the focus of the second unit in the chapter. The activities in this unit ask students to recreate several facets of Billy's hunting episodes. Those activities, in turn, provide students with ideas which they can later use in their own writing. The unit culminates with students taking a hunting trip of their own—a camera safari on which they can either "shoot" their game with a camera or sketch pictures of the animals they hunt. After finishing the hunting trip, students will have notes on the chronology of what they did, when, and where; mental and written descriptions of their animals; and notes describing their emotions while searching for and when catching (or never catching) their game. These notes become material for their own stories.

A baseball story, Carl Deuker's *Heart of a Champion,* is the third unit in the chapter. Deuker naturally incorporates the excitement of baseball into the story of two friends. In this unit, students use the sport of baseball to explore the friendship between Seth and Jimmy as well as their own feelings about relationships and about sports. Students examine various aspects of baseball, including its colorful jargon, design their own baseball cards, and write their own action-packed sports stories.

Writing With Master Storyteller Jan Cheripko

Voices of the River: Adventures on the Delaware

Composing Strategies Highlighted

1. Using sporting experiences as a writing source

2. Keeping journals

3. Recording a journey in pictures

4. Writing with a friend

5. Revising with an editor

Background Information

Jan Cheripko writes books for young people. He also works with at-risk teenagers. In *Voices of the River: Adventures on the Delaware,* Cheripko recounts in words and pictures a 215-mile canoe trip that he and a 14-year-old friend, Matthew Smith, took in the summer of 1992. The ten-day trip, which began at Hancock, New York, and ended at Philadelphia, Pennsylvania, taxed the physical and emotional stamina of the voyagers. Unforgiving weather, difficult terrain, and unknown dangers around every bend created daily thrills and trials.

Cheripko and Smith discovered that the river, while dangerous in some spots, is also beautiful and is a rich source of information about natural and political history. Readers learn about trout fishing on the Delaware River; about the habits of eels, shad, blue herons, mute swans, eagles, and wild ducks; about eddies, chutes, sandbars, and various classifications of rapids based on their difficulty; about the changing color of water as it gets deeper or shallower or gathers various vegetation or pollutants. Readers learn about historical figures, famous and obscure, whose lives touched the banks of the Delaware—figures such as western author Zane Grey; John Augustus Roebling, builder of the Brooklyn Bridge; Chief Joseph Brandt, who fought for the English during the Revolutionary War; and President George Washington, who gained victory for the colonies when he led the Continental Army across the Delaware River. Readers learn about the role of reservoirs and dams for supplying water and controlling floods; about the Appalachian Mountain chain and the Lehigh River; about the habits of people who live along the Delaware now; and about the lives of those, like the Lenni Lenape Indians, who lived there in the past.

This range of information in the *Voices of the River* photo journal gives teachers the opportunity to integrate disciplines. History, biology, sports, ecology, physics, earth science, geography, political science, and language arts come together naturally as students travel along the river with the writers, learning from the "voices" of the Delaware River.

Voices of the River provides a unique writing model for students, appealing to students interested in nature and sports. It shows that athletes can also be good writers. Besides enjoying canoeing, the author, 41-year-old Jan Cheripko, is a former football linebacker. His co-author, 14-year-old Matthew Smith, enjoys playing basketball, fishing, jet-skiing, and motorbiking. Like Cheripko and Smith, students can use their sports experiences as catalysts for writing. In *Voices of the River,* students see that, not only does athletic activity promote physical fitness and mental acuity, but it can even be the subject of the writing itself.

The excerpts included in this unit give some of the flavor of the trip, showing Cheripko and Smith setting off on their trip and later negotiating unexpected rapids. Cheripko provides day-to-day, even hour-by-hour, details of the trip apparently writing from notes taken on the trip and arranging and revising them later during reflection. Although Cheripko writes the bulk of the finished narrative, Smith writes both the introduction and the epilogue, sharing his initial fears and candid assessment of the experience. Excerpts from Smith's reflections on what he learned on the trip are also included in this unit, as is a map of the journey from the origins of the Delaware in New York to its confluence with the Atlantic Ocean at Philadelphia, Pennsylvania.

Students can use Cheripko and Smith's collaboration as a model for writing their own photo journals. They can plan substantial journeys or even short excursions with friends or family—camping trips, bike trips, or hikes—collecting details during the trip by making journal entries and taking pictures. Later, like Cheripko and Smith, they can edit their journal entries to create an illustrated chronicle of the journey.

Included in this unit is a manuscript page from an early draft of *Voices of the River* with the author's revision plans and his editor's recommendations. After students identify changes and discuss the motivations for and effects of those changes, they can work with one another to edit their own work. Rather than limiting their attention to spelling and mechanics choices, students can see in Cheripko's drafts that revision involves a whole range of actions, including addition, deletion, and rearrangement. Through these collaborative experiences in which key issues are negotiated, students learn some of the essential strategies of good writing.

Voices of the River: Adventures on the Delaware, by Jan Cheripko (1993), is published by Caroline House, Boyds Mills Press, A *Highlights* Company, Honesdale, Pennsylvania.

Getting to Know *Voices of the River: Adventures on the Delaware*

In *Voices of the River: Adventures on the Delaware,* 41-year-old Jan Cheripko and 14-year-old Matthew Smith write about their ten-day, 215-mile canoe trip on the Delaware River. To preserve the details of their experience, they captured events in pictures and daily journal entries, creating a photo journal of this adventure. This map shows the route that the two canoers traveled from Hancock in the upper left to near Philadelphia in the bottom right.

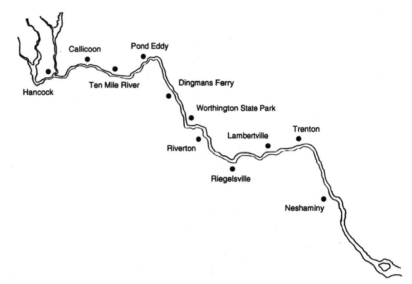

The Fascination of Rivers

Voices of the River begins with an introduction by Matthew, who admits that he had doubts about whether he would enjoy the trip. But he thinks it is important to try to do things that are new and difficult.

> At first, I wasn't sure I wanted to go. I didn't want to spend my whole summer canoeing and miss basketball camp. . . . It turned out that the trip could be done in ten days if everything went right. I could still go to basketball camp. I think my father helped convince me to go on the trip. He told me that he wished he'd had a chance to do something like this when he was a kid. He told me that I would remember this trip for the rest of my life. . . . My father told me that the river would teach me something. He was right. . . . I learned that there are a lot of things to do out there, a lot of possibilities in life.

1. Would you have been nervous about going on a ten-day, 215-mile canoe trip? Why or why not?_____

Later Matthew admitted that the trip wasn't always fun, but he learned a lot, especially about himself.

> I learned a lot about frustration—the way to get past it is to keep on doing whatever you're doing. No matter what it is, keep doing it. . . . I learned something important about myself—I am not a good beginner, but once I start something, I'll see it through to the end. . . . One last thing. When you spend ten days with someone, ten days paddling a canoe for eight to ten hours a day, you don't always get along. And that's okay.

2. When have you tried something that was new and difficult? Was it a valuable learning experience? _____

Chapter 1: Planning the Trip and Setting Off

Cheripko and Smith discovered on their journey that the river, while rich in natural beauty and political history, could also be very dangerous. Following is the first page of Chapter 1, "Rain, Trout, and an Eagle—From Hancock to Callicoon," in which Cheripko outlines the plans for the trip and shares the excitement and concern that he and his companion felt about the adventure.

A wet, soggy mist hung over the river. Gray and black clouds floated above us as Matthew and I carried our seventeen-foot Grumman aluminum canoe down to the Delaware at the tip of Point Mountain near Hancock. Like the fog-draped world around us, we were wrapped in hazy dreams. We weren't thinking that this was the first day of a long, long journey. Or if we thought about it at all, we didn't know how far 215 miles really is, or how long ten days on the river will last.

I thought to myself, "Oh well, we're going canoeing. We'll have a nice time."

Starting something you've never done before isn't easy. You feel a lot of confusion. Your body rushes forward with excitement ready to get going, but your mind holds you back with its warnings that hard work and danger lie ahead.

Having people around helps you get started, at least that's the way Matthew and I felt. It would have been hard to say, "I've changed my mind. I don't want to go." But we both certainly thought about not going, right up until we shoved off.

It was July 5, 1992. We planned to pull our canoe out of the river ten days later at Neshaminy State Park, a few miles north of Philadelphia.

But this was Day One of our trip. With Point Mountain watching over us, we walked across the grassy field, past clumps of small riverbank trees, and down the dirt path dropping sharply toward the river. Ahead of us, the Delaware roiled and gurgled.

At the point where its east and west branches slide into one another, the Delaware River is about a football field wide from bank to bank. It's filled with a smattering of rapids, deep pools, and dark channels. This morning, after days of on-and-off rain, the Delaware ran fast and strong at the start of its long journey to the Atlantic Ocean.

1. Why do you think Cheripko and Smith wanted to make this long and dangerous journey?

   _____

   _____

   _____

2. A lot of people are fascinated by rivers. Many movies, songs, and stories reflect this interest. Think of as many movie, song, and story titles as you can. On the blackboard, list all of the titles that the class can name.

   _____

   _____

   _____

3. Write a journal entry about your own experiences with some river or other body of water.

   _____

   _____

   _____

4. Bring to class (a) pictures of rivers or other bodies of water and (b) tapes with songs about rivers (for example, Carly Simon's *Let the River Flow).* Look at the pictures, and while listening to the music, write a story that includes a river. Describe the scene, characters, and situation.

Writing About Jan Cheripko's *Voices of the River: Adventures on the Delaware*

Comparing the First and Second Drafts of Chapter 1

Voices of the River did not start out exactly the way you see it in the book. Below is an early draft of the beginning of Chapter 1, along with the editor's comments. Working in pairs, compare the two drafts by placing pages 28 and 29 side by side. On a separate sheet of paper, tell (1) what differences you see, (2) which draft you prefer and why, and (3) whether you agree with the editor's suggestions and why.

3

CHAPTER ONE

Rain, Trout, and an Eagle - From Hancock to Callicoon

Having a lot of people around when you start something helps make you start. At least that's the way Matthew and I felt, ~~when we started~~. It would have been hard to say ~~to everyone,~~ "I've changed my mind. I don't want to go."

But we both certainly thought about not going. There was a lot of excitement that first day. We carried our canoe and equipment down to the river at the tip of Point Mountain near Hancock. A photographer snapped pictures of us as we pushed our seventeen-foot Grumman aluminum canoe into the water at the exact spot where the East and West Branches of the Delaware River meet.

A wet, soggy mist hung over the river, and gray and black clouds floated above us. It was July 5, 1992. Ten days and 215 miles later, we planned to pull our canoe out of the river at Neshaminy State Park, a few miles north of Philadelphia. We were both in a dream world. You don't think about how far you're going. You just think, "Oh well, we're going canoeing. We'll have a nice time."

It's all new and exciting. You just have no idea that this is the first day of a long, long journey. Or if you think about that at all, you don't know how far 215 miles is, or how long ten days on the river will last.

Less than an hour after we pushed off it started to drizzle, and soon it was pouring straight into our faces. Even though we didn't say it, I know we both were thinking what a

Manuscript reproduced courtesy of Jan Cheripko and Boyds Mills Press

Revision Choices

Sometimes students think revision means correcting words and punctuation, but professional writers know that the most important revision involves ideas. Most revisions fall into one of three categories: addition, deletion, and rearrangement. Again working in pairs, find at least one example of each in Cheripko's Chapter 1 drafts. Try to find passages, rather than simply words, that have been changed and list them on the lines below. Identify each passage by listing either the idea contained in the passage or the first four words. On the blackboard, compile a class list of the changes you find.

Additions	Deletions	Rearrangements
_____	_____	_____
_____	_____	_____
_____	_____	_____
_____	_____	_____

Editor's Early Draft Recommendations

Below are some of Cheripko's editor's reactions to an early draft of *Voices of the River.*

1. What kinds of things did the editor like?

_____
_____
_____

2. What recommendations did he make for improvement?

_____
_____
_____

Chapter 8: Thrills and Dangers in the Rapids

In Chapter 8, "A Day with Kayakers, Then a Surprise—From Riegelsville to Lambertville," Cheripko describes some of the thrills and dangers on the ten-day journey. Although all rapids present a challenge to canoers, some are more dangerous than others. In this section, Cheripko refers to the rating of rapids—from easy to difficult—with "Class I" being the easiest. Look to see whether you think Cheripko took his editor's advice in writing and revising this section.

The Delaware has three wing dams: at Lumberville, Lambertville, and Scudders Falls. The wing dams were built in the 1800s to help the rafters by creating small lakes to store the rafts in until they were ready to go over the rapids. Some creative and courageous local people would charge to guide the rafts through the rapids. In later years, the wing dams were reinforced with concrete to create small reservoirs for drinking water.

The wing dams can be dangerous. If the river is high, and you go over the dam, you can get trapped in the water below the dam. It's like a whirlpool. The rushing water keeps holding you down. Even if you have a life jacket on, there's a good chance you'll drown.

It would be important for us to go through the center chute of the dam. There was a Class I Plus rapid at the chute's center. We weren't too worried about the rapid, but we didn't want to go over the dam.

. . . Then suddenly we saw it. Or, really, we didn't see it. The river that is. It just dropped out of sight. We both realized what was happening. The water was higher than we had thought it would be, maybe from rain upriver. Whatever the reason, the river was going over the wing dam! And we were heading right for it.

We should have been out in the middle looking for the chute. Instead, we were staying near shore away from the jet skis, and now we were fewer than forty yards from the dam.

"Oh no!" Matt cried out as he raised himself up to see over the dam.

"Cut to the right!" I yelled.

We cut hard and paddled toward the center chute. Now we were sideways to the current, and the river was pushing us towards the dam. There are television shows that capture real-life rescues on video. Often those rescues are of people trapped in rivers. And sometimes, the people who are trapped were over just this kind of a low wing dam. Looking back on it now, I realize that we were very lucky. If we had gone over the dam sideways, there's no telling what could have happened to us.

Ten yards from the dam we shot into the rapid. Right in front of us were the biggest waves we had seen. Bigger than Skinners Falls, bigger than Mongaup, bigger than Foul Rift. They were close to four feet high, and we were headed right into them.

The river grabbed us and jerked us forward.

"Here we go!" Matt cried.

"Keep paddling," I yelled.

My heart pounded furiously as I beat at the waves.

"No more rapids!" Matt yelled back.

"We're gonna make it!" I shouted, though I was sure we were going to be swamped.

We shot up one wave, down the other side of it, and then hurtled into another that raged over our heads. I heard Matt cry out, "Oh no!"

Somehow, and I don't know how, we made it through the center chute without capsizing. We fought our way through the rest of the rapid. Silently, we headed towards shore at Bull's Island, the Lumberville wing dam a bad memory behind us.

Cheripko's Writing Process

Cheripko described the process of writing this book. Below, he talks about writing Chapter 8.

The challenge for me was to combine expository writing with narrative writing. Each of my ten chapters includes several paragraphs which tell readers what Matthew and I are doing. At the beginning of Chapter 8, for example, I write, "We slid through the morning haze down the steep bank in front of the Riegelsville Hotel to our canoe. I think I could have slept another three hours, and I know Matt could have, but we were getting anxious to finish the trip." By writing in the first person, I try to help the reader envision what we're doing. A couple of paragraphs later, however, I need to tell the reader some information about the Delaware River, so I switch to exposition: "The Delaware has three wing dams: at Lumberville, Lambertville, and Scudders Falls." The information that I then disclose about these wing dams is critical to understanding the story line. We came close to going over one of the wing dams, but I couldn't advance the plot unless I first told the reader what a wing dam was. . . . I also did something else in the style of writing, which, technically speaking, a good reporter would not do—I used the familiar "you." While my writing about the facts is expository, I do it in a conversational tone, hoping that the reader will relate to the facts about the river and the dam and not be bogged down by them.

1. What information about the wing dams was new to you? How did it help you understand the predicament of the canoists?

   _____

   _____

2. From the passage on page 31, choose one paragraph that uses first person (*I*, *we*, or *us*), and rewrite it to make it straight exposition, like the paragraphs about the wing dams. What is the effect of removing the familiar pronouns and using third person terms like "the canoeists" or "they"?

   _____

   _____

3. Cheripko's second paragraph on page 31 uses "you." Again, rewrite this paragraph using third person to see what happens when you remove the conversational tone.

   _____

   _____

Later in that same chapter, I tell about Matthew and me hitting the first wing dam and almost going over it. Here, I rely on strong, active verbs, and personification of the river. . . . And I use dialogue to bring the reader into the immediacy of the action. . . . Both the use of short active verbs and of dialogue are techniques I picked up as a sports writer. Pick up any city-wide or national newspaper, check out the sports pages, and you'll discover the same techniques. . . . And on almost every sports story, there will be interviews with the winners and losers. Again, readers like to know what the characters think about the event. It gives readers an opportunity to identify in the struggle.

4. From the Chapter 8 passage on page 31, find and list five strong, active verbs.

5. Find at least two examples of personification of the river.

6. What is your reaction to the dialogue in this passage? Does it speed up your reading or slow it down?

Writing With Jan Cheripko

Borrowing From Newspaper Sports Writing

Having started his own career as a sports writer, Cheripko offered the following advice to beginning writers:

I think some of the best non-fiction writing being presented today can be found on the sports pages of newspapers. A good sports writer knows how to bring the reader into the event, present the necessary facts in a clear and concise manner, weave a good story line, and present believable and interesting protagonists [main characters] and antagonists [main characters' opponents] by developing the characterization of the players of a game. Sports lends itself to literature, because it already has the necessary elements for a good story—beginning, middle, and end, and conflict and resolution. A game is the perfect vehicle for a story, because it is a story itself. All the reporter has to do is tell the story, highlighting the most interesting points and capturing the human drama of the event …

The same techniques that I learned as a sports writer and that I tried to use as a photojournalist in *Voices of the River* I employ in my new book *Imitate the Tiger,* a young adult novel about a high school football player who has a drinking problem. In the novel, I [use inner dialogue] to explore more deeply the thoughts that a character might have. Thus, . . . the reader is invited to identify even more strongly with the people and the plot of the story. One night, the main character, Chris Serbo, and his best friend, Billy Krovats, sit on a park wall drinking, and Chris asks Billy about when his father left his family. Billy tells Chris, matter-of-factly, that he came home from a Little League game one night, and he discovered his mother crying. She told Billy his father was gone, and here's what Chris says to himself: "I thought about that for awhile. I can see Billy standing there in some kitchen in some house in another town in another lifetime. I can feel the pain that stabs you when you're left alone and the only person to help you is your mother, and she can't, because she's shriveling up to nothing right before your eyes. There is no one to hold you. No one to tell you that they love you. You just stand there alone, and she cries."

Obviously, there is more that a writer can do in developing a character in a novel or even a photojournal, but the approach is similar: Tell a good story that has a clear beginning, middle, and end, create a conflict for the protagonist, offer a plausible and exciting resolution, develop believable and captivating characters, and do it all with clear, detailed, precise, and poetic language. That's easier said than done.

1. Find a sports story in a newspaper to use as the basis for your own newspaper story, creating rival characters and a plot with a beginning, middle, and end.
2. Write some dialogue for two of your characters.
3. When you have a complete draft, get another writer to read your story and offer suggestions.
4. Share your original newspaper story and your "revision" with the class.

Taking Notes From a Fictional Journey: *The River Wild*

Watch the movie *The River Wild.* Take notes and make sketches as though you were actually on the trip. Try to capture details about water, mountains, birds, fish, and weather, as Cheripko and Smith did in *Voices of the River.* Take these notes as day-by-day entries, dating them as you would if you were entering them each day as they occurred. Although the story line about the criminals is interesting, focus more on the natural elements and the canoeing difficulty—that is, focus on the main characters' struggle with nature rather than their struggle with the two criminals. Stop the film or reverse it as necessary to help you give your journal entries full details. Use your notes and sketches to create your own short version of *The River Wild.*

Creating Your Own Photojournal

1. Like Cheripko, plan a journey with a special friend. Your journey can be a canoe trip, camping trip, bike trip, fishing trip, or even a hike. Matthew said that canoeing was not his only, or even his favorite, sport but the difficulty of it taught him something. Like Matthew, you may want to try something new. Before you go, do some research so that, like Cheripko, you will be able to include a wide range of information about the area—historical events, people, habits of animals, geographical features, etc.

2. Create a detailed map of the intended trip.

3. Take notes during the journey. Record hour by hour events, including details about anything interesting that you see. For example, if you go on a fishing trip, you can observe and research the plants and animals on the banks and in the water. You can describe the bridges, the texture of the soil, other people fishing, boating, or just enjoying the scene. You can describe your fishing lures and your success, or lack of success, with each. Be sure to listen to the sounds, or "voices," of the river and write about those.

4. Take pictures and make sketches that help tell the story. If you do not have a camera, sketch pictures of your observations, or find pictures in magazines that show the kinds of things you observed.

5. Using your notes, map, journal entries, and pictures, work with your friend to compile the first draft of a photojournal of your trip. You may want to divide up the work by writing separate chapters or sections, or you may want to write it all together. Include pictures on every page.

6. Reading each other's papers is an important part of the writing process. Because you know your own paper so well, you cannot judge whether it is clear to a reader. Pair off and serve as each other's editors. Like Cheripko and his editor, give each other feedback that includes specific examples of what you like and what you think could be improved.

7. Publish the finished photojournals by reading them aloud to the class. Bind the stories in illustrated covers and place them in the class library.

Alternative Journeys

If you cannot take a real journey, you could gather materials from a vacation you have taken in the past, arranging photographs and writing down details about the trip. For example, if you visited the Grand Canyon, provide information about the origins of the Canyon, the inhabitants of the area, the types of plants and animals found there, the difficulties of traveling into it, and so on.

Another alternative to an actual trip is a walking tour of your school. You could take pictures of students, staff, parts of the building, facilities, the grounds, and the adjacent community. Your story could be directed toward people who know nothing of your school, or it could be directed to classmates to point out—humorously or seriously—strengths and shortcomings of the school.

Writing With Master Novelist Wilson Rawls

Where the Red Fern Grows

Composing Strategies Highlighted

1. Finding and solving problems in literature

2. Recreating sites, objects, and activities as an impetus for writing

3. Conducting a camera safari to generate writing ideas

4. Writing about a hunting experience

Background Information

Born September 24, 1913, Wilson Rawls spent the early years of his life on a farm in northeastern Oklahoma. Since there were no schools in that area, his mother taught him and his sisters how to read and write. A book she read aloud, Jack London's *The Call of the Wild,* deeply impressed Rawls. In fact, Rawls recalls it as his first real treasure, a treasure which inspired him to want to write a similar book. Rawls did attend school regularly after the family moved to Tahlequah, but he never finished eighth grade since the family once again moved—this time because of the Depression. However, lack of money and a formal education did not prevent him from writing. He remembers his first writing as words scratched out.

Rawls worked many jobs, including carpentry and construction. He also worked on an Alaskan highway, on five major dam projects in the United States, in shipyards, for the Navy, and for a lumber company. Most of these jobs required manual dexterity. For relaxation, he loved to fish and hunt, again kinesthetic activities. Rawls would write during his spare time but often felt inadequate as a writer because of poor grammar skills.

Rawls burned all of his manuscripts before he got married, perhaps because of the feeling of inadequacy. The manuscript of *Where the Red Fern Grows* and the manuscripts of four other novels were destroyed at this time. With his wife's encouragement, Rawls later rewrote *Where the Red Fern Grows,* a story based on his boyhood life. The *Saturday Evening Post* serialized the story in three parts, using the title *Hounds of Youth.*

Rawls serves as a model of a person who had a poignant story to tell but who was hindered by problems with grammar and spelling. He did not allow his weaknesses to prevent him from telling his story. Rather, he remembered his father's advice that a man can reach his goal as long as he does not give up, knowing that writing means telling a good story, not just getting down "correct" words and phrases.

Many middle school students may feel like Rawls—that they have talents and consequently stories to tell but that they do not have the verbal skills to tell those stories well. The activities in this unit will use the kinesthetic skills of the sport of hunting as a basis for writing. Students will recreate some of the experiences Billy has during the course of the novel to help them generate material which they can use to write about the novel. Students will then organize and go on their own hunts; however, they will "shoot their game" with cameras rather than hunt with an ax as Billy did. The kinesthetic movement of actually conducting the camera safaris and the developed photographs give students a wealth of ideas to incorporate into their own writing. Coupled with prehunting notes and notes taken during and/or after the hunting trip, students become well-equipped and able to write their own stories.

Getting to Know Wilson Rawls's *Where the Red Fern Grows*

Problem Finding

Many problems face Billy during the course of the novel. Several are listed below. In small groups, write why each was a problem for Billy. Then rank the problems in order, 1 being the most serious problem facing Billy.

_____ 1. Billy does not have money to purchase dogs.

_____

_____

_____ 2. Billy gets his dogs from Tahlequah.

_____

_____

_____ 3. Billy must acquire the first coon hide to train Little Ann and Old Dan.

_____

_____

_____ 4. Billy needs to figure out where the Ghost Coon is hiding.

_____

_____

_____ 5. A blizzard rages during the last night of the Championship Coon Hunt.

_____

_____

Problem Solving

Choose a problem from the previous page. Jot down facts that relate to the problem. Not all questions will have specific answers.

Problem:

Who? _____

What? _____

Where? _____

When? _____

How? _____

Why? _____

How does Billy solve this problem?

_____

_____

_____

_____

In small groups, evaluate Billy's solution. What is the impact of Billy's solution?

_____

_____

_____

_____

Writing About Wilson Rawls's *Where the Red Fern Grows*

Recreating Billy's Hunting Episodes

Billy knew the geography of the land around his home. Because of this knowledge, he had little fear of the area and did many things that worried his mother. Choose one or more of the following to recreate:

1. Billy decided to walk to Tahlequah, approximately 30 miles, to get his dogs. On the return trip, he camped in a cave with his dogs only to get worried when he heard the cries of a mountain lion. Build (or draw) a campsite which includes a cave. Make a list of provisions you would bring with you. What would you bring to carry your two puppies? Remember, you must be able to carry everything. Write about your trip. Include a thorough description of the campsite.

2. Billy's grandfather showed him how to build a trap that would not kill a coon. Reconstruct this trap or construct one of your own. Be certain that the animal caught in your trap would not be injured or killed. Write a paper telling how to build this trap. Be certain to include necessary materials and step-by-step directions.

3. Billy used a coon hide to train his dogs. He dragged the hide over ground, up trees, and through bushes so that the dogs could practice following the scent. Create a trail of your own. You may wish to drop miniature marshmallows, Cheerios, or other small items along the way to represent the "scent." Have a classmate follow your trail, but be certain that you do not require him or her to do anything physically dangerous. How long does it take your partner to complete the trail? Write about your partner's problems and successes. Have your partner write about his or her problems and successes. Did you both notice the same things?

4. When Little Ann and Old Dan tree their first coon, Billy is both excited and dismayed. He is thrilled because they have learned their job so well, but the dogs have treed the coon in the largest sycamore in the area. Afraid that he cannot chop down the tree, Billy knows he cannot let down his dogs. He chops all night, but the tree does not come down. Finally, Billy's grandfather has a plan. He says that a scarecrow will fool the coon for at least four to five days. Make this scarecrow. In writing, describe your scarecrow. Why and how would it effectively keep a coon in the tree?

Making Ethical Decisions

Divide the class into groups of three to four students each. Discuss and take notes on the following situations:

1. Grandfather helps Billy fashion a trap using nails in a funnel shape and bright, shiny objects. Knowing the habits of coons, Grandfather knows that the coon will reach for the shiny object and will not be able to get its paw past the nails because it will not let the object go. Billy's father tells him to destroy the traps he used to catch the first coon because such traps are not sportsmanlike. Yet Billy later hunts and kills many coons. Why does Father feel Billy should not use the nail traps? Why does he allow Billy to kill coons with his ax? Do you agree with Father's decisions? Why?

2. In the story, Billy hunts for the pleasure of it. He gives the hides to his grandfather and gives the money from the hides to his father. Although he knows the price of hides has skyrocketed because of the desire for raccoon fur in the East, Billy forgets about the money as soon as he turns it over to his father. Should animals be killed to provide humans with fur hats or coats? Should animals be killed to provide humans with leather belts, shoes, wallets, etc.? Why?

3. Billy's dogs tree the Ghost Coon, but Billy cannot kill it, even after a grueling hunt. Rather, he lets it go to the disbelief and ire of Rainey and Reuben. Do you agree with his decision? Be certain to give reasons for agreeing or disagreeing.

Write a persuasive paper concerning the issue of hunting (and killing) animals. Establish a stance, either for or against hunting, and give reasons why others should agree with your opinion. Incorporate some ideas from your small-group discussion into your paper.

Writing With Wilson Rawls

Going on a Camera Safari

Where the Red Fern Grows is a story of a boy and his two dogs. Together, they form a unique hunting team. For your final project, you will conduct your own hunting expedition. Like Rawls, you will then have a hunting experience to develop into a story.

1. Decide on an animal to hunt. Study that animal's appearance and habits, and the tracks it leaves in the dirt, mud, or snow.

2. Draw a map depicting where you will hunt your game. You may add markings for your possible path.

3. Take a camera and snap pictures of evidence you find that shows the animal has been there. You may include tracks, nests, eating habits, and other physical evidence.

4. When you spot the animal, take its picture.

5. Along your trek, jot down notes about your adventures. Describe the time of day during which you are hunting and the weather. What are your feelings as you hunt? How do you feel immediately after "shooting" your animal?

6. Develop the photographs.

7. Mount the developed photographs on display paper and write short captions for each picture.

8. Write a short narrative about your hunt. Try to remember the events in chronological order.

9. Create a title for your camera safari.

Capturing the Camera Safari on Paper

Write a hunting story based on your experiences from your camera safari. You may write the story from a first-person point of view as Rawls did, or you may write it from a third-person point of view.

Include in your story at least three episodes. Remember, although Rawls wrote from his boyhood experiences, his novel is fiction. Feel free to embellish, change, or add to the actual events and feelings you experienced. Begin your first draft here.

_____
title

_____
_____
_____
_____
_____
_____
_____
_____
_____
_____
_____
_____
_____
_____
_____
_____
_____
_____
_____

Writing With Master Novelist Carl Deuker

Heart of a Champion

Composing Strategies Highlighted

1. Using sports to generate story ideas

2. Finding ideas in personal relationships

3. Recreating game situations to generate vivid language

4. Using game situations, statistics, and jargon to draft a short story

5. Writing to capture personal relationships and plot action

Background Information

Carl Deuker has written two outstanding sports stories for young adult readers. His first, *On the Devil's Court,* deals with basketball, and his second, *Heart of a Champion,* is about baseball. As a physical education teacher, Deuker has spent much of his life involved in kinesthetic activity. Being involved with physical education on a daily basis inspired Deuker to incorporate the art of sports into words. Deuker knows the importance adolescents place on sports. In fact, for many students, athletics is their primary interest. Sports can also spark their interest in the academic areas.

Many students dedicate hours each day to practice and perfect such kinesthetic movement as hitting a well-timed spike in a volleyball match, achieving hang time while shooting a jump shot in basketball, developing the rhythm of jumping hurdles in track, or putting the final touches to a modern dance routine. While the choreography and performance of dance most naturally corresponds to a written composition, the ability to use both fine and gross motor skills in any sport offers yet another talent which students can tap to enhance their writing skills. Students who excel at sports may find they learn best when they use movement to solve problems or to create something.

Kinesthetic learners often use movement for expression; however, the athlete's "composition" is his or her performance in a game. Unlike the composer of a song, the artist of a painted canvas, or the author of a written text, the athlete usually creates his or her composition by changing, revising, refining, or perfecting in practice, prior to presenting the finished piece. The performance of the "text" includes both impressive moves as well as mistakes. This combination merely adds to the excitement of the game or "composition."

Baseball, often referred to as the great American sport, incorporates athletic skill, teamwork, and the contest itself to produce its art form. Baseball, in the form of T-ball, introduces many youngsters to organized sports. Yet baseball not only requires fine and gross motor skills, it also demands use of vivid language, a specialized jargon, and knowledge of its rules. The appearance of baseball in literature goes back to 1888 when Ernest Lawrence Thayer brought us *Casey at the Bat*. Although mighty Casey failed to save the day, he nevertheless lives on in the minds and hearts of young and old alike. In the early 1900s Ring Lardner created a baseball character named Jack Keefe, and the list continues with such memorable works as *Shoeless Joe* by W. P. Kinsella, upon which the movie *Field of Dreams* was based. The jargon, legends, statistics, and action of the game excite millions of fans each year in parks and museums from the ivy of Wrigley Field in Chicago, Illinois, to the National Baseball Hall of Fame in Cooperstown, New York.

In this unit, students will use sports activities to generate ideas for writing. Teamwork, dedication, and sacrifice make up traits to which both athletes and writers can relate. Students will examine both the game of baseball and personal relationships to acquire ideas for their own stories. The activities in this unit lend themselves ideally to an integrated unit with physical education and mathematics classes. Students can play baseball or softball games in physical education class, figure their batting averages and other statistics in mathematics class, and design their baseball/softball/sports cards in language arts class.

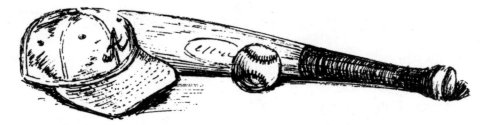

Getting to Know Carl Deuker's *Heart of a Champion*

The Influence of Sports on Characters

Heart of a Champion is the story of two friends who love the game of baseball. To both Seth Barham and Jimmy Winter, baseball becomes more than just a game; it influences other facets of their lives and even helps to shape their personalities, defining who they are as people. In small groups, discuss the following situations, jotting down notes as group members consider various aspects of the situations.

1. In Part II, Chapter 1, Greg Dayley cheats during summer pick-up games. However, Seth refuses to allow Greg to run the baseball field, and he stands up to Greg. In Part II, Chapter 3, Jimmy wants Seth to lie about his address so that they can play on the same team. Seth's mother tells Seth a story about his father, who refused to golf with a man who cheated. Seth says that his situation is different, but his mother refuses to relent. Discuss the two situations. How does cheating affect the pick-up games? How would Seth's participation on the Belmont Braves team have changed that team? What does Seth's mother teach him by not allowing him to lie about his address?

2. Reread Part II, Chapter 2. In this chapter, Jimmy teaches Seth to concentrate on the baseball field. Without realizing it, Seth begins to concentrate more in the classroom. On what types of things must Seth, as a baseball player, concentrate? On what types of things must a student in a classroom concentrate? How does concentration help Seth in the classroom?

3. Todd Franks, the best hitter on the team, does not buy into Coach Sharront's coaching style. He soon gets some followers who start dogging it at practice. When Todd disobeys the coach's signal, he gets benched. Infuriated, he quits. Later, when Jimmy joins the team, he beats Coach in the two-mile, after-practice run and becomes the leader of the team. His outfield chatter is catching, and the other players begin to practice harder. Discuss how one person can influence the attitude and performance of other individuals and of the success of the team as a whole.

4. In Part III, Chapter 1, when the coach moves Seth down to the junior varsity team, Seth believes the way to work back up to varsity ball is to hit the ball. He becomes concerned only with his batting statistics. In a game situation, Seth does not look at his coach because he knows he will see a "take" sign. Rather, Seth hits a home run. Upset, Coach Blackman benches Seth and Coach Sharront talks to him about his attitude and about being a team player. What does being a "team player" entail? Does attitude affect performance, performance affect attitude, or both?

Name _____

Analyzing Personal Relationships: Fathers and Sons

Seth's father died when Seth was seven years old. Jimmy's father is alive, but during the course of the novel, he divorces Jimmy's mother. In your small groups, discuss the following:

1. Jimmy's father insists he use a new glove, even though it hurts Jimmy's hand; he forces Jimmy to take a ball "off the chest;" he continually corrects Jimmy's mistakes; and he yells at the umpires.

2. Even after Jimmy's father moves out of the house, Jimmy still credits his ability and success to his father.

3. Jimmy says that when his father is around, he wants him to go away; but when his father stays away, Jimmy wishes he were around.

4. Seth's mother understands his passion for baseball and at times helps him practice. At one point, she tells Seth that he was like his father who worked at being "the best lousy golfer in the world." Seth understands that comment late in the novel when he realizes that he could never be a major league player but that he could work to be the best high school player possible.

5. Seth and his mother occasionally experience times when the absence of Mr. Barham is quite painful. Even at the end of the book, Seth states that his father should be there to see him play ball.

After Jimmy experiences problems with Mr. Winter, Seth often thinks about his own father and his death. At one point, Seth wonders whether it is better to have a father like Jimmy's or none at all. What do you think? In what ways does Jimmy's father help and/or hurt Jimmy? In what ways does Seth's mother compensate for Seth's loss of a father? Write your answers here. Then discuss them with your group members.

_____

_____

_____

_____

_____

_____

Name _____

Writing About Carl Deuker's *Heart of a Champion*

Friendship

Throughout the novel Seth and Jimmy are close friends. Among the problems that confront their friendship are Jimmy's moving, Seth's being in honors classes, Jimmy's being the star of the team, and Jimmy's drinking problems.

Recreate the dialogue between Seth and Jimmy. You may act out the scene(s) if you wish. Select from the following:

1. varsity tryouts in Part II, Chapter 20 and the conversation between Seth and Jimmy after Seth gets cut from the varsity team
2. the conversation in Part IV, Chapter 5 in which Seth confronts Jimmy about his drinking
3. the game situation in Part IV, Chapter 7 in which Jimmy tells Seth to get on base
4. the conversation between Seth and Jimmy in Part IV, Chapter 8 in which Jimmy asks Seth to write a term paper for him

Write a paper comparing and contrasting the two characters in this story. Use the conversations from the above activity as well as the chart below. One section of the chart is blank so that you can add an additional category of your choice.

	Seth	Jimmy
Fathers		
Baseball Ability		
School		

Writing With Carl Deuker

Using Your Kinesthetic Ability to Generate Ideas

Writing is often difficult. People with kinesthetic talents may find writing easier when they base their stories on activities in which they participate. Try one or more of the activities below. On another sheet of paper, try to describe exactly what you do in the activity and jot down answers to the questions which follow the activity.

1. Throughout the book, Seth's main problem is his inability to hit a fast ball. When Seth purchases new equipment, the salesman encourages him to buy a lighter bat, but Seth wants a heavier one like Jimmy's. Later, Jimmy gets Seth a new bat, one that is 32 inches long but weighs only 28 ounces. Try hitting a ball with a heavy bat. Then try hitting one with a lighter bat. What are the results? What other problems do players often face? How can they improve these problem areas?

2. Like Seth and Jimmy, play a game of pickle, pepper, or wiffle ball—or modify baseball's rules and create a game of your own (give the game a name). How does your modified game help you become better at the official game? Or is it a game you play just for fun? What is the value of such games?

3. Jimmy's father was a baseball player; Seth's father earned many trophies in golf. Play a round of golf or play a few innings of baseball. Do you like playing golf or baseball better? Why?

4. From your experience of either playing or watching baseball or golf, jot down some of the specialized jargon associated with either sport. For example, how many terms can you think of for a home run? A lengthy list will provide a colorful, exciting repertoire of words and phrases which you can later use in your original sports stories.

Creating Your Own Sports Card

Sports fans have collected baseball cards for years and have prized cards of certain heroes. In recent years collecting baseball cards has become more than a young boy's hobby; it has become a serious business. In Part I, Chapter 9, Seth writes down his baseball stats in a notebook. He plans to make a baseball card of himself at the end of the season. However, after Steve Cannon strikes him out, Seth thinks he was foolish and tears up the statistics.

Like Seth, design your own baseball card. Use statistics from at least five games—games played in physical education class, the school baseball or softball teams, or the community baseball or softball teams. On the front of the card attach a picture. On the back fill in the appropriate information. The statistics may be calculated in math class. When you finish, laminate your card. If you prefer, design a card depicting statistics from another sport of your choice.

(picture)

Name _____
Team _____
Position _____

(front)

Height: _____
Weight: _____
Hometown: _____

Bats (right/left/switch)
Throws (right/left)

Statistics:
at bats _____
hits _____
runs _____
base on balls _____
strikeouts _____
average _____

(back)

Play Ball!

In *Heart of a Champion,* Seth tries to understand life (and death) through writing down the story of baseball, of Jimmy, and of himself.

1. Using your notes from the "Influence of Sports" activity (page 45), your responses to the kinesthetic activities, and the information from your sports card, write the first draft of your own story.

2. Ask group members for suggestions and make any revisions you think are necessary. Like Deuker, be certain to include both human relationships and sports in the plot.

3. Add scenarios from game situations to your story where appropriate. You may wish to include individual players' statistics or team statistics. Remember colorful jargon used in the game.

4. Compile your stories in a classroom anthology called "Sports Shorts."

MUSICAL ABILITY

Few things interest people more than music. A poll of any group of people would reveal strong musical tastes. Whether it is classical, western, jazz, romantic, pop, or rock, most people are "tuned in." This affection for music is not a new phenomenon. Ancient cultures preserved stories through songs, often using crudely-fashioned musical instruments similar to drums, flutes, and stringed instruments to accompany them. The instruments frequently imitated bird songs and other sounds of nature. In fact, music was thought to have magical powers, as in the chanting of rain dances. Anthropological studies of primitive cultures living today reveal that music continues to be an integral part of their lives, helping them in their work and entertaining them in their leisure.

Music is also a mode of communication. Like language, it has meaning and can convey ideas and feelings through sounds and rhythms. Compare, for example, the sounds of horses' hooves galloping along the trail in a soundtrack from a western movie and the sounds of nature in a pastoral symphony. Even without words, these two pieces of music generate different interpretive responses in the listener. Musical notation, of course, is actually a language with its own set of signs. The musical sign system used today developed over a period of at least a thousand years. The five-line staff with each space and line representing notes on the scale, the treble and bass clef signs, the notes themselves representing different time values, the time signatures and key signatures, along with innumerable performance terms, all convey essential information to the musician reading them.

An increasing number of research studies have shown that sounds—particularly rhythmic sounds—have great educational and even therapeutic value. In several studies, students receiving regular music instruction in piano or voice—and in some cases simply listening to music—raised their IQ scores and outscored their peers significantly in tests of spatial reasoning. In fact, music has even been credited with generating rhythmic responses from autistic children and bringing people out of comas.

The connection between music and spoken language is especially apparent in theatrical productions, in poetry, and in song lyrics, which are really poems set to music. But the connection extends much further than this. The human voice itself is musical. It has cadence, timbre, pitch, rhythm, accent, and so on. In fact, musical instruments are designed to work very much like the human voice. When we speak, our vocal cords vibrate, and, along with actions in the mouth and throat, the vibration helps us to form different sounds, pitches, and intensities. Musical instruments work on similar principles. Violins, pianos, drums, and wind instruments, for example, create vibrations or force air through mouthpieces.

Practice in making meaning with music enhances students' ability to make meaning in other ways as well. The connection to writing is especially important. A musical composition, like a story, essay, or poem, has a beginning, middle, and end. The listener knows when the piece begins without an appropriate introduction and senses when it ends too abruptly. In each instance, the listener sets up expectations and makes predictions, predictions which are confirmed or revised as the piece continues. The units in this chapter attempt to tap into these common qualities of music and language to expand students' knowledge and ability in both areas. Because most students already have a strong appreciation for music, the integration is a natural and pleasant way to enhance their abilities as readers and writers.

Selections from Emily Dickinson's poems comprise the first unit in this chapter. Dickinson's great fondness for nature, whose voices she imitated in her poetry, provides readily accessible subjects and models for student writing. Her practice of borrowing freely from other writers' poems and stories provides yet another useful strategy. The intensely rhythmic quality of Dickinson's poems helps students to see clearly the music in poetry and, to some extent, in all spoken language. Because Dickinson provided very few titles for her poems (most are identified simply by their first lines) students have an opportunity to provide their own titles, and, thereby, to make thematic statements. Similarly, because the poems printed here are from Dickinson's original manuscripts, students engage in actual word and punctuation decisions that confronted Dickinson and her editors.

The Magician's Nephew, by C. S. Lewis, is the focus of the second unit. This unit gives students the opportunity to think about how music enhances creativity. Student writers discuss the symbolism of lions and the sounds that lions and other animals make. The "music" of these sounds becomes the basis for helping student writers investigate their own emotional responses to various kinds of music. These emotional responses lead to drawing and writing about musical preferences and experiences. Students then return to their own preferred animals as representatives of kinds of music and have the opportunity to consider how personal feelings can evoke different musical and written compositions. Finally, writers respond to one another's choices and compositions.

John Steinbeck's *The Red Pony* concludes the chapter on music and orality. In recent years, teachers have begun to recognize the importance of oral language activities in the development of students' reading and writing skills. Students are asked to imitate Grandfather in the book, reciting their own family legends and then writing about them. Furthermore, Steinbeck's revising practice involved reading his manuscript into a recording machine and listening to what he had written. Once again students can imitate Steinbeck's practice, reading their own stories into a tape recorder and listening for strengths and weaknesses. The culminating project is a series of related stories that, like *The Red Pony,* recall childhood events, places, and people.

Writing With Master Poet Emily Dickinson

"The Bee Is Not Afraid of Me," "The Morns Are Meeker Than They Were" "A Narrow Fellow in the Grass," "I'm Nobody! Who Are You?" "This Is My Letter to the World"

Composing Strategies Highlighted

1. Using song lyrics to understand the "music" of poetry

2. Finding rhythm and meter in poetry

3. Finding images in poetry

4. Finding subjects in the sights and sounds of nature for writing poetry

Background Information

Emily Dickinson probably holds the distinction for the poet having the largest number of poems set to music. More than two hundred composers, including such well known names as Aaron Copeland, are known to have written music for her poems, for everything from solo voice and piano to opera and ballet with full orchestra. Some composers have made her poems the major focus of their life's work.

The attraction of Dickinson's poetry for composers is that they reflect Dickinson's extraordinary ear for sound and rhythm. The poems are concise, compact, and lyrical, often written in the common meter of alternating eight-syllable and six-syllable line lengths, typical of many hymns. In fact, Dickinson often called her poems "hymns." The poems communicate inner thoughts, universal themes, and emotional force through striking metaphors and musical word sounds. Her sharp images, drawn with simple, direct language lend themselves to rich and varied interpretation through musical voices. Although Dickinson clearly had a natural ear for music, she also had an impressive musical education. Her training included lessons in piano and voice, including instruction and practice with church music.

Her interest in poetry began at a very early age. Apparently it was her custom to find poems in books, magazines, and newspapers, and then rewrite those poems. Sometimes she would borrow a plot element from a story, place herself in the story (or a persona using "I") and write a poem as though she were herself a character in the plot. Her imitations or revisions of these poems ranged from classical to popular poems, both American and English.

Themes of nature, death, life, and immortality pervade her poetry. Madness, irrationality, hypocrisy, brutality, despair, anger, love, loss, and acceptance are frequent subjects. She had an especially deep love for the natural world. She wrote about birds, bells, bees, butterflies, sunsets, and other everyday subjects, as well as spiritual elements. Her poems often begin with an observation about some minute feature of the natural world and, as the poem progresses, applies that observation to a larger truth. Particulars in the natural world point beyond the world of mortals to truths in the spiritual world.

In both style and subject matter, many of Dickinson's poems are indistinguishable at first from her prose. The line lengths often cover the width of the page in her poems, and her prose often looks and reads very much like poetry. Some poems were later rewritten in prose, and lines in letters would emerge later as poems. Some of the earliest poems were valentines. Like modern greeting cards, these poems served to convey condolences or congratulations, offer regrets for not writing, or simply confirm friendship.

Although she avoided public view for a period of years, Dickinson was not unmindful of the world around her. Her reluctance to publish her poems may have had much to do with editors' eagerness to "revise" the unconventional style of her poems. Although she sought reactions to her poems, she was adamant about keeping control of her verses. On numerous occasions, she reflected on the possibilities and responsibilities of fame. In fact, two of the poems in this unit reflect her ambivalence about the subject. "I'm Nobody! Who Are You?" suggests that she prefers to be unheralded, whereas "This Is My Letter to the World" reflects a distinct concern for her public image.

In the lessons in this unit, students are invited to see the extensive knowledge they already have about poetry by looking at song lyrics as poems set to music. Like Dickinson, who often referred to her writing of poetry as "singing," students can look at poems as song lyrics, adding appropriate musical voices through instrumentation. After some practice with basic techniques of prosody, as well as a review of some musical terms, students will write their own poems both for reading and for singing. In setting poems to music, students learn that form needs to enhance—even help to convey—the meaning of the poems. When used in addition to conventional readings, setting poetry to music offers an expanded perspective from which students can appreciate the poem, especially the role of rhythm.

Like Dickinson, students will draw subjects from reading and from nature as they create their own original poems. They will revise other writers' poems, incorporate poetry lines in letters, create metrical patterns for poems, and create their own greeting-card letters, showing that even poems can be written for real people in real situations.

Because the poems printed in this unit have been taken from Dickinson's original manuscripts, they look different from most anthologized versions, which have been edited in various ways. Dickinson's unconventional capitalization and punctuation and her lack of titles offer students yet another way to gain insights into the types of decisions that authors and editors must make.

Getting to Know Emily Dickinson's Poetry

Music All Around Us

Most of us take the music around us for granted. Because it is so much a part of our lives—beginning with lullabies and nursery rhymes—we may not realize how much we depend on it to make our lives meaningful. We have special music for holidays, and music for movies, dancing, games, and listening moods. Even if we are only listening, we do not do it passively. We whistle or hum, tap our feet, dance, or sing along.

"The Bee Is Not Afraid of Me"

Emily Dickinson used this universal fondness for music in writing her poetry. She listened to the sounds around her and wrote about them in rhythms that could be set to music. In fact, she often referred to her poems as songs, and hundreds of them have actually been set to music by famous composers. To generate ideas for her poetry, Dickinson closely observed the world around her. Her poetry is especially rich with the sights and sounds of nature—bees, frogs, birds, butterflies, snakes, and even leaves and grass blowing in the wind can be heard and seen in her poems. As you read the lines below aloud, look for words that create sounds and pictures. Try to imagine how a musician would suggest the activities of each plant and animal.

The Bee is not afraid of me.
I know the Butterfly.
The pretty people in the Woods
Receive Me Cordially—

The Brooks laugh louder
When I come.
The Breezes Madder play
Wherefore Mine eye thy silver mists,
Wherefore, Oh Summer's Day?

1. Working in pairs or small groups, list at least six words or phrases that suggest sounds or pictures. Describe how you would play this part of the poem musically. What instrumental voices would you use (piano, flute, violin, harp, clarinet, drums, trumpet, etc.)? What tempo, volume, and rhythm would you use (fast/slow, loud/soft, smooth/staccato, etc.)? What human voices would you use (single voice—soprano, bass, etc.—a few voices, or a full chorus made up of only men, women, children, or mixed)?

Word or Phrase	Instrumental Voices	Tempo/Volume/Rhythm	Human Voices
_____	_____	_____	_____
_____	_____	_____	_____
_____	_____	_____	_____
_____	_____	_____	_____
_____	_____	_____	_____
_____	_____	_____	_____

2. Dickinson's poems rarely have titles. In fact, very few were published before she died. When editors took them from handwritten manuscripts, the poems were identified simply by the first line. What title would you choose for the poem above? Pick one that captures the meaning of the poem for you. _____

Making Music With Metrical Patterns

Although you may not always recognize it, poetry has its own inner music. In fact, Dickinson often used metrical patterns similar to those used in hymns. Try singing "The Bee Is Not Afraid of Me" to this melody from a seventeenth century hymn.

Making Music With Meter

Both musicians and poets pay a lot of attention to line length (the number of syllables) and patterns of stressed (accented) and unstressed syllables. In poetry, two syllables—usually one stressed and one unstressed—are called a *metric foot*. See whether you can determine the metrical pattern for "The Bee Is Not Afraid of Me."

1. Count the number of *syllables* in the first line. _____

2. How many *metrical feet* are in this line? _____

3. How many *metrical feet* are in the second line? _____ the third? _____
   the fourth? _____

4. Now read the poem aloud to determine which syllables are stressed and which are unstressed. (If you have difficulty deciding whether a syllable is stressed or not, try singing it again. You will quickly see where you place the accented beat.) Mark the *stressed* syllables with an accent mark like this ´ and the *unstressed* syllables with a mark like this ˘.

5. Do you find that the unstressed syllable comes first or second in each foot? _____
   (If you counted right, you should have found that, exactly like the seventeenth century hymn above, Dickinson used alternating lines of eight syllables and six syllables–four feet and three feet–with the unstressed syllable coming first in each metric foot.)

6. Choose a favorite song with a regular metrical pattern. Write your own words to fit the melody. Make certain that your words are suitable for the music. For example, you would not use a sing-song melody for a serious subject unless you meant to treat the subject humorously.

7. Dickinson often wrote poems from her prose pieces, but she also wrote prose pieces from her poems. Find some interesting song lyrics and turn them into a story by adding details.

Making Music With Sounds

"The Morns Are Meeker Than They Were"

Another way that poets make music is with sounds. The rhyme at the ends of lines is easy to see, but there are important repeating sounds within the lines too. Read the following poem aloud:

The morns are meeker than they were—   The Maple wears a gayer scarf—
The nuts are getting brown—   The field a scarlet gown—
The berry's cheek is plumper—   Lest I sh'd be old fashioned
The Rose is out of town.   I'll put a trinket on.

1. Where do you find end rhymes? List the word pairs.

   _____

2. Where do you find repeating sounds within the lines (repetition of "s" or "m" for example)?

   _____

3. See whether you can identify the metrical pattern of this poem. Is it the same as or different from "The Bee Is Not Afraid of Me"? _____

4. In this poem, Dickinson observes the colors of the seasons. What season is this, and how do you know?

   _____

   _____

5. Poems have emotional tones or moods (happy, sad, angry, playful, etc.). How would you describe the mood of this poem? Why?

6. What title would you give this poem? _____

7. Dickinson started out writing poems by revising other people's poetry. She found poems that she liked in books and magazines and then revised them to make them her own. In fact, many famous writers learn to write well by imitating other writers' work. Try your hand at "revising" this poem by changing the season. Keep any of Dickinson's words that will fit in your revised version. Try to maintain the metrical pattern. You might even see if you can make it rhyme. Give your poem a title and share it with the class.

   _____

   _____   _____

   _____   _____

   _____   _____

   _____   _____

Writing About Emily Dickinson's Poetry

"A Narrow Fellow in the Grass"

As you have seen, Dickinson's poetry shows her great fondness for nature. You have read about plants, insects, and seasons. Below she writes about an animal. Work in groups to see whether you can identify it.

A narrow Fellow in
the Grass
Occasionally rides—
You may have met Him—
did you not
His notice sudden is—

The Grass divides as
with a Comb
A spotted shaft is
seen—
And then it closes
at your feet
And opens further on—

He likes a Boggy
Acre
A Floor too cool
for Corn—
Yet when a Boy, and
Barefoot—
I more than once at
Noon

Have passed, I thought,
A Whip lash
Unbraiding in the Sun
When stooping to secure
it
It wrinkled, and was
gone—

Several of Nature's
People
I know,
and they know
me—
I feel for them a
transport
Of Cordiality—

But never met this
Fellow
Attended, or alone
Without a tighter
breathing
And Zero at the Bone—

1. What have you decided it is?_____What is your evidence?_____
2. How does the speaker feel about this animal?_____What lines tell you?_____
3. Could the speaker be talking about people too? Have you ever known anyone who could be called "a snake in the grass"? What does that mean? Write about your experience with snakes.
4. Is the metrical pattern similar to or different from that in the poems on pages 55 and 57? (You cannot tell by looking because, even though the spacing changes, the meter may stay the same. Try singing it to the hymn on page 56.)

Using a Persona

Dickinson liked to write poems about things she read. Often she would write as though she were a character in the story. Although she often used the pronoun "I," she did not intend for the reader to think she was writing about herself. Instead, she was doing what writers often do—she was writing as though she were someone else. This is called using a *persona*. In "A Narrow Fellow in the Grass," she wrote, "when a Boy … I more than once … " Obviously, she was never a boy, but she was using the *persona* of a man recalling his boyhood. Find an interesting story or news report and write a poem in which you adopt a *persona,* pretending to be a character in the story.

Name _____

Editing Dickinson's Poems

"I'm Nobody! Who Are You?"

Some editors of Dickinson's poems were distressed by her unconventional spacing, meter, rhyme, punctuation (they much preferred commas to dashes), and certain words that seemed odd or ill-chosen. These editors often changed the poems to conform to more conventional standards. Dickinson's original manuscripts show the following poem spaced, capitalized, and punctuated as you see it here. Pretend you are Dickinson's editor. Revise the punctuation, capitalization, spacing, line lengths, indentions, etc. to make it look more traditional. Do you like it better? Why or why not?

I'm Nobody! Who are you?	How dreary—to be—Somebody!
Are you—Nobody—too?	How public—like a Frog—
Then there's a pair of us!	To tell your name—the livelong
Dont tell! they'd banish	June—
us—you know!	to an Admiring Bog!

1. The manuscript of "I'm Nobody! Who Are You?" shows that Dickinson could not decide whether to use *banish* or *advertise* in line four. *Banish* was written in the line, but *advertise* was written beside it, suggesting that Dickinson added it later. Most editors use *banish,* but because she had not crossed out *advertise,* we don't really know what her final choice was. Which one do you like better? What difference does it make? A similar problem occurs in line eight. The manuscript shows *your* written in the line and *one's* was added later. Editors commonly use *your.* Which one would you choose if you were the editor?_____

2. What title would you give this poem? _____

3. "I'm Nobody! Who Are You?" probably came from a poem Dickinson read in the newspaper that included the line, "Who would be a Somebody?—Nobody am I." Choose a line from one of Dickinson's poems to use as the main point of your own two-stanza poem. Use conventional spacing, capitalization, and punctuation, or be daring, like Dickinson, and create your own style.

"This Is My Letter to the World"

1. People who have studied Dickinson's work and her life are not sure what she thought about the possibilities of becoming a famous poet . Based on your reading of "I'm Nobody! Who Are You?" and the following poem, what do you think about her desire for fame?

This is my letter to the World	Her Message is Committed
That never wrote to Me—	To Hands I Cannot see.
The simple News that Nature told—	For love of Her—Sweet—Country-
With tender Majesty	men
	Judge tenderly—of Me

2. A large musical production of "I'm Nobody!" was performed humorously with a jazzy sound and a chorus that made frog-like sounds. What kind of music would you use for "This Is My Letter to the World"? _____

What would you title it? _____

Writing With Emily Dickinson

Writing About Nature

Listen to the sounds and observe the sights of the world around you, as Dickinson often did. In the country, listen for the sounds of farm machinery and livestock. In the city, listen to the sounds of cars, trains, buses, planes, church bells, school bells, and lawn mowers. Listen to wind, rain, thunder, ocean waves, frogs, birds, crickets, dogs, and cats. Look at sunsets, flowers, rivers, trees, and animals of all sorts. Write a poem using some of these sounds and sights. You may want to imitate Dickinson's "A Narrow Fellow in the Grass" describing something that can apply both to nature and to people. You may also want to follow Dickinson's metrical pattern.

Writing Greeting-Card Letters and Poems

Many of Dickinson's poems originated as lines in letters. Like modern greeting cards, they offered congratulations or condolences, told receivers that they were missed, or confirmed friendships. Some of her earliest poems were really valentines. Dickinson used the term *medley* to describe the lines in a valentine that she had written to a gentleman friend. Look up the word *medley*.

- Write a lengthy valentine poem that can be described as a medley.
- Write a letter to someone, enclosing an original poem with an appropriate greeting.

Adapting Poetry to Music and Music Lyrics to Poetry

1. To see how much we rely on music without realizing it, play a scary movie scene without sound. Then play the same scene with sound. How does the fear level change?

2. Singing a poem changes the reader's/listener's experience. Try this experiment to see whether the music makes a difference for you.
   - Choose a song whose lyrics you especially like. Read the lyrics as though they were a poem, and write your interpretation.
   - Listen to the song on tape. Revise your interpretation.

3. To see how the form of a poem or song affects how you read it, try the following:
   - Lay the song lyrics out on the page as though they were a poem.
   - Experiment with spacing, punctuation, and capitalization to emphasize different key words.
   - Read each version aloud.

4. Poems actually have stories implied, even if they are not actually stated. Song lyrics do too, as in ballads. But even instrumental music has hints of stories—movie soundtracks for example. Because the composer always arranges sounds in a particular order, with one part leading to another, like a story, there is always a beginning, middle, and end. Try "reading" different types of instrumental music.
   - Listen to three different types of music.
   - As you listen to each piece, write a short narrative. Describe the characters, plot, and setting.
   - Write a theme statement and illustrate each story. Compare your "readings."

Creating Poetry Anthologies

Revise all of the poetry exercises in this unit. Get feedback from other students, but before making changes, be certain you agree with the advice. Create a poetry booklet of original and revised poems. Build a class anthology of poetry. Include pictures of yourselves as poets, and include brief biographical notes.

Writing With Master Storyteller
C. S. Lewis

The Magician's Nephew

Composing Strategies Highlighted

1. Using singing to evoke feelings for writing

2. Creating an imaginary new world

3. Using animal noises (voices) and human needs as a basis for writing

Background Information

Ancient philosophers talked of the music of the spheres, referring to the systematic and predictable movement of the planets and constellations through the heavens. So systematic was the movement of these bodies that these ancient philosophers argued that the movements "sounded" musical in their mathematical precision. C. S. Lewis used this ancient concept to create a wonderful fictional scene. Lewis, known to many readers for his famous *The Chronicles of Narnia,* also holds an outstanding scholarly reputation as an expert on the seventeenth century and the Medieval Romance era. His scholarly books, especially *The Allegory of Love* and *Studies in Medieval and Renaissance Literature,* detail a world view that assumes order in both science and society. That order can be noted in the music of those times because Medieval and Renaissance music both contain measured dance forms and stately chants and liturgies for church services—music that assures the listener that the universe moves to a set rhythm.

Lewis's scholarly interests centered on a universe created by a rational and logical deity, one best represented in the predictability of musical sounds. Music itself is mathematical in that it has predictable intervals between notes and measurable rhythms and cadences. Lewis would have argued that one need only look at the wonderful structure of any piano or organ keyboard to see the orderliness of the natural world as it is represented in music. For Lewis, the universe truly did reflect the organized and structured music of the spheres.

When Lewis set out to write his Narnia tales, he began with the image in his head of a great golden lion, whom he later named Aslan. Some think that the lion may resemble the golden retrievers who succeeded one another as a constant part of Lewis's home life. At any rate, as Lewis spun out the stories, each tale became more tightly connected with the lion of Narnia. As readers will remember, Aslan died, an innocent and willing sacrifice for a wrongdoer, in the first and most well-known of the volumes, *The Lion, the Witch, and the Wardrobe.* He, of course, came alive again shortly after his execution. Throughout the tales, Aslan reappears to save and direct the various children as they pursue their adventures in Narnia. Aslan finally becomes known as the creator of all of Narnia in the next to the last volume, *The Magician's Nephew.* There the boy Digory (a pretty clear version of the young Lewis) and his Uncle Andrew accidentally find themselves back in time at the creation of Narnia. Digory hears a noise, not quite music yet, but the most lovely noise imaginable. It is the great lion singing. As he sings, the world of Narnia comes into being. In some of the most wonderful pages ever written (99-107), Lewis tells of each stage of Narnia's creation, each part responding to a different part of the song. When the song ends, the new world has begun.

In this unit, students will learn how to use music to create their own worlds, using music to connect with writing, drawing, and motion. The unit offers many options so that both students and teacher will be comfortable with their classroom music.

The Chronicles of Narnia by C. S. Lewis

Lewis, C. S. *The Lion, the Witch, and the Wardrobe.* New York: Collier Books, 1970.

—. *Prince Caspian: The Return to Narnia.* New York: Macmillan, 1988.

—. *The Voyage of "The Dawn Treader."* New York: Macmillan, 1988.

—. *The Silver Chair.* New York: HarperTrophy, 1994.

—. *The Horse and His Boy.* New York: HarperCollins, 1994.

—. *The Magician's Nephew.* New York: Macmillan, 1988.

—. *The Last Battle.* New York: Macmillan, 1988.

Getting to Know C. S. Lewis's *The Magician's Nephew*

The Power of Song

C. S. Lewis tells the story of Narnia by beginning in the middle. When he began to write the first book, he did not know that it would be the middle. He started to tell a story about a wonderful lion named Aslan. The story turned into a tale about some children who travel into a parallel world, Narnia. After Lewis had written five books about that world, he wrote a sixth that would explain where the parallel world began. That story became *The Magician's Nephew*. In it, the lion "sings" Narnia into being.

As the lion sings different notes, different parts of the world come into being. Low notes bring about Earth, high notes the sun. The music moves the adults and children who listen to it in various ways depending on their personalities. The good or innocent characters, including an old cart horse, feel lively and happy when they hear the music. The selfish and bad-tempered characters despise the music and want to get away from the new world as quickly as possible. When they cannot escape, the worst-tempered of them all, Jadis, hurls a lamppost at the lion. That lamppost glances off the lion's forehead and roots in the ground, becoming, of course, the lamppost that Lucy will later, or actually earlier in the first book, find in Narnia.

1. Lewis chose a lion to be the creator of his world. Write down as many words as you can think of to describe lions:

_____   _____

_____   _____

_____   _____

_____   _____

_____   _____

2. Lewis loved golden retriever dogs. Why would he choose a lion rather than a dog as the creator of his imaginary world? In a group, discuss why it is important that the animal who sings the creation song be a lion. Write a list of your reasons below.

_____

_____

_____

_____

3. How do you feel when you hear a lion roar on television or in a movie? What does a lion's roar usually mean, or at least what do you imagine that it means? Write down words to describe your reactions to the word "roar."

_____

_____

4. Lewis believed that writers were "creators" of the stories that they wrote. Thus he was creating the Narnia tales in the same way that Aslan was creating Narnia, and he was creating a mood in his readers as he wrote the pages describing Narnia's beginnings. Describe how you feel when you read Lewis's story. Compare your feelings to music that you know. Write about your feelings below.

_____

_____

_____

_____

_____

_____

Writing About C. S. Lewis's *The Magician's Nephew*

Focusing on Song

1. Lewis admired stories about Vikings and Norse people (early settlers of England and Germany from places that are now Sweden, Denmark, and Norway). In the "North" tales, words and letters were very significant. Runes (letters) could have powerful meanings. When letters were worked together into poems and put to music, they became powerful forces in the community. Singers of songs, or *scops*, were honored when they came to visit with their harps on their backs. Thus it is not surprising that Lewis had a singer create his imaginary world.

   List some songs that you find particularly important to you, either personally or as "public" symbols (for example, the national anthem).

   _____

   _____

   _____

   _____

   _____

2. Lewis also felt that music represented the closest human connection possible to the order and structure of the universe. Draw a diagram or picture of the solar system of our galaxy as you imagine it to be, or use a model that you find in a science book.

3. Ancient writers thought that the spheres made music as they moved across the sky. In a small group, discuss what kind of music you imagine the planets would make as they move around the sun. Would the music sound like a roar, or maybe a purr, or even a growl, or something else? Describe your group's ideas below.

_____

_____

_____

_____

_____

4. Music can "create" moods in people. Bring to class tapes or CDs that you like. If possible, ask your teacher to find tapes of famous inspiring music like the national anthem. Then write about how the music makes you feel.

_____

_____

_____

_____

Compare your impressions of each song with those of your classmates. List the similarities and differences.

_____

_____

_____

_____

_____

Writing With C. S. Lewis

Choose Your Creature

We all have our favorite animals—or even fantasy creatures. Those creatures can have great power for us, sometimes becoming symbols of important events in our lives. Certainly, mascots have powerful meaning for sports teams, and many people find that they cannot imagine life without a favorite pet. Lewis felt this way about his golden retrievers and somehow translated his love for these animals into the lion. He then combined that love with his scholarly knowledge about the way ancients viewed the creation of the universe. He put the two together in a wonderful story.

Try your own combinations in the activities below.

1. Describe your favorite pet, animal, mascot, or wild animal below. Draw a picture of it on the back of this page and write about it below.

_____
_____
_____
_____
_____
_____
_____
_____
_____
_____

2. Imagine the "song" that this animal would sing. Would it be popular music, folk, or some other type of song? Describe the song, writing as much of it as you can.

_____
_____
_____
_____
_____

3. What sort of world would your animal create? Would it be a better world than the one we live in now? Lewis's Aslan creates a world in which all animals live together peacefully and where they can talk to one another. Perhaps your animal's world would reflect something about the nature of the animal. Describe it below.

    _____
    _____
    _____
    _____
    _____
    _____

4. Put your animal and your favorite kind of music together. Write a story about your animal's world. Compare your stories with those of others in your group or class. Write about your reactions to a friend's animal and song.

    _____
    _____
    _____
    _____
    _____
    _____
    _____
    _____
    _____
    _____
    _____
    _____
    _____
    _____
    _____
    _____
    _____
    _____

Writing With Master Storyteller John Steinbeck

The Red Pony

Composing Strategies Highlighted

1. Writing about people, places, pets, and events in your life

2. Storytelling as a thinking and writing strategy

3. Using listening as a revising strategy

4. Creating vivid visual and aural experiences in writing

Background Information

Few stories touch our hearts the way *The Red Pony* does. The character Jody, who longs to ride his pony in the Salinas rodeo, is based on Steinbeck's own experiences as a child when he too wanted to ride his pony, Jill, in the rodeo. The ranch in the story is based on property homesteaded by Steinbeck's grandparents near King City, California, a ranch where Steinbeck sometimes spent summers with relatives. Jody and others in the novel speak for many people who long for times past or dreams unfulfilled, a common theme in Steinbeck's works. The novel's immense popularity in the public schools is evidence of its enduring worth.

The Red Pony is comprised of four separate, but related, stories. The stories create sharp images with great economy of language. The prose has a symphonic quality, conveying emotions and ideas in clear, direct, and lyrical prose, a style that no doubt comes partly from Steinbeck's attention to the sounds of language. The fourth story, "The Leader of the People," introduces the grandfather, who likes to tell stories of pioneering adventures. Students imitate Grandfather by doing some storytelling of their own, enhancing both their reading ability and their writing skills. Like reading, storytelling requires listeners to participate actively by creating mental pictures, forming hunches and modifying them as the story proceeds, tapping prior knowledge, and monitoring their own understanding of the story. As the storyteller relates personal experiences, listeners recall similar experiences of their own and, thereby, create new understandings, both of the storyteller's narrative and of their own life experiences.

A particularly important reason for including storytelling in a language arts class is that some oral/aural learners, who sometimes perform poorly in written language activities, excel in speaking and listening skills. By developing these students' oral language experiences through storytelling, teachers can help them tap their ability with oral texts to use in the production of written texts.

Oral language development is overlooked in many classrooms where teachers do the talking and students are encouraged to be quiet. But teachers have an important resource in the students' own speaking experiences. When teachers model storytelling by sharing their own legends, students begin to see their life experiences as rich repositories of materials for writing. They gain insights, not only into other people's lives, but into their own as well.

Steinbeck's revision strategies suggest an especially valuable strategy for students who are aural learners. Apparently, Steinbeck not only wrote multiple drafts, but he also made multiple recordings. Once he had a draft, he read it aloud into a tape recorder. Then he played it back so he could hear what he had written. What he didn't like, he would change. Each time he revised it, he would record it again and listen to the sounds of his story. He claimed that hearing the story aloud enabled him to hear clearly the most obvious and most subtle faults in his drafts. Steinbeck said he was not able to get the same effect from reading aloud because the involvement of the eyes distracted him from the sounds of the story.

The activities in this unit ask students to analyze the experiences of characters in the story and then write about similar experiences in their own lives. Like Steinbeck, they record their stories and listen to them on tape. Like Grandfather, they tell episodes from their own histories and family legends and revise the narratives in response to their audience's responses.

Steinbeck on his red pony, Jill
Courtesy of the Steinbeck Archives of the Salinas Public Library, Salinas, California

Name _____

Getting to Know John Steinbeck's *The Red Pony*

Getting to Know Characters

All four stories or episodes in *The Red Pony* tell about the experiences of four characters: Jody Tiflin, his mother Ruth Tiflin, his father Carl Tiflin, and the ranch hand Billy Buck. Gitano is added in the second story, "The Great Mountains," and Grandfather is added in the fourth story, "The Leader of the People." When a writer creates characters, the characters are almost always based on real people. Sometimes a character is a "composite," including qualities of several people the writer has known, but the habits, appearance, behavior, and values reflect real people with universal qualities that readers recognize from their own experiences with similar types of people.

1. In the chart below, describe each of the characters in *The Red Pony*. Use adjectives such as proud, sensitive, wise, kind, tough, dreamy, inventive, practical, mean, gentle, respectful, fearful, etc. Back up your character descriptions with examples from the book. Then describe someone you know who has similar traits. Discuss your character descriptions with others.

Character	Description	Text Evidence	Someone You Know
Jody			
Billy Buck			
Ruth Tiflin			
Carl Tiflin			
Gitano			
Grandfather			

2. Pick at least one of the people from your "Someone You Know" list and write a paragraph about your experience with this person. Try to choose a person and an experience that you think might make an interesting character in a story.

Including Details in the Setting

A lot of a story's details are missed the first time you read it. To check your attention to detail in *The Red Pony,* circle any of the animals in the following list that you think Steinbeck included in the story. (Check your answers on the bottom of page 73.)

antelopes	deer	mules	roosters
bats	dogs	newts	sheep
birds	fleas	nighthawks	snakes
blackbirds	gophers	oxen	squirrels
buffalo	grasshoppers	pigeons	steers
buzzards	hawks	pigs	ticks
calves	hoot owls	pony	toads
cats	horses	quail	turkeys
chickens	lambs	rats	
cows	lizards	rabbits	
coyotes	mice	roadrunners	

1. Not only did Steinbeck use a lot of animals in *The Red Pony,* but the details show that he observed the animals closely. List and briefly describe several animals whose habits you know fairly well.

   Animal   **Habits**

   _____   _____
   _____   _____
   _____   _____
   _____   _____
   _____   _____

2. Write a paragraph about your experience with one of these animals.

3. In the third story, "The Promise," Jody talks about special places. The black cypress tree makes him feel bad and frightened, but the water tub makes him feel peaceful, and it makes him feel better to go there when he is upset. Describe and draw a special place for you, one that you go to when you want to feel better. If there is a place that you find frightening, or one you found frightening when you were younger, describe and draw it, too.

4. We tend to think of a story's setting as things you can see, but *sound* is part of a setting too. Jody hears his father's and Billy's footsteps and knows whether they are wearing boots or shoes; he hears the sick pony's breathing; he hears the hame bells on a team of horses; he hears the barn door screech when he goes to the barn in the night—a sound he never heard in the daytime; and on his walk home from school, he imagines he is marching at the head of an army troop with drums and trumpets sounding. Write a paragraph about an experience you have had that involved sounds. Like Jody, you might think of people's footsteps, animal noises, sounds from games, or eerie noises you have heard in the night.

Name _____

Writing About John Steinbeck's *The Red Pony*

Writing About Plot and Theme

1. Notice that each of the stories in *The Red Pony* has its own plot and theme. In fact, you could read any one of the stories by itself. You could even change the order of some of the stories. Working in small groups or pairs, briefly tell in the spaces below what each of the stories is *mainly* about. (Tell it the way you would tell a friend very briefly about a book or movie: "It's about a boy who … ")
    "The Gift"

    _____

    _____

    "The Great Mountains"

    _____

    _____

    "The Promise"

    _____

    _____

    "The Leader of the People"

    _____

    _____

2. Now try to think about the *meaning* in the stories. That is, what point or points do you think Steinbeck had in mind? What might he have wanted his readers to see about *the way life is?*
    "The Gift"

    _____

    _____

    "The Great Mountains"

    _____

    _____

    "The Promise"

    _____

    _____

    "The Leader of the People"

    _____

    _____

(All of the animals listed on page 72 were used in the book.)

Name _____

Reading and Listening Actively

If you are an active reader or listener, you usually recall experiences of your own when you read or hear about someone else's experiences. You also predict what is going to happen to characters and even imagine outcomes that the author does not include. Read through the questions below under each story title. Choose one question from each story, and briefly describe your own experience or your predictions about the characters' further experiences. Circle the number of the question you are answering.

"The Gift"
1. Before the pony came, Jody had a hard time getting out of bed when the triangle sounded. After the arrival of the pony, he got up long before it rang. Have you ever had a gift or an activity that excited you enough to make you want to get up early?
2. Jody's red pony was very precious to him. Describe a pet that you have had or that someone you know has had, and tell of an incident involving this pet. For example, you might tell how or when you got it or, like Jody's pony, you might tell about a time when it was "bad."

_____

_____

"The Great Mountains"
1. Sometimes Jody did mean things. For example, he hit birds or dogs needlessly. Jody's father was also mean sometimes. When have you intentionally done something you now consider mean? Why do you think you did it? How did you feel then? How do you feel now?
2. We do not know what happened to Gitano before he arrived at the Tiflin ranch, nor do we know what happened to him after he left with Easter and his sword. Write Gitano's story. Where had he been and what had he done? What happened to him after he left the Tiflin ranch?

_____

_____

"The Promise"
1. Jody dreams of winning first place in the Salinas rodeo and helping the president catch bandits in Washington. What heroes did you pretend to be when you were young?
2. The story ends with Billy handing Jody the colt. Finish the story by telling what happened to Jody and the colt in the following months and years.

_____

_____

"The Leader of the People"
1. Jody's grandfather says that people aren't interested in pioneering—or "westering"—anymore. Do you know anyone who still has the westering spirit?
2. Jody likes to hear Grandfather tell stories about the pioneers and Indians. What stories do your parents and grandparents tell over and over again?

_____

_____

Writing With John Steinbeck

In this unit you have written several paragraphs about the stories in *The Red Pony* and about your own experiences. As a final project, put some of these paragraphs together to create your own autobiographical collection. Or, if you prefer, write sequels to the stories in *The Red Pony*. Like Steinbeck, write a series of four stories on a related topic.

Storytelling

Before you begin writing, try storytelling. Telling or reading stories out loud helps both the writer and the listener think of new ideas and consider an audience's needs. Tell the class some of your family legends. If you do not immediately recall any, ask your parents to help you. You could even tell stories about your own childhood. As classmates tell their stories, you will find that you recall similar stories of your own. Jot these recollections down. Be an active listener. Ask questions when you think the storyteller has left out important information.

Creating Story Collections and Sequels

Topics

Autobiographical Collection. If you choose to write about your own experiences, select ideas and passages from the paragraphs you wrote in response to prompts on pages 71, 72, and 74 (someone you know, animal descriptions, special places, sounds, gifts or pets, mean acts, hero games, and family stories). Part of Steinbeck's book came from his experiences with his own pony, Jill. As a child, he wanted to ride in a rodeo, so he included this detail in his book. Because Steinbeck was very interested in family legends, he included those in his writing, too. Like Steinbeck, you can write about your childhood, your pets, and your family's legends.

Sequel Collection. If you choose to write sequels to the stories in *The Red Pony,* use your paragraphs on page 74 (Gitano's story in "The Great Mountains" and the story of Jody and the colt in "The Promise") in writing two of your stories. Add to these your sequels to "The Gift" and "The Leader of the People." Tell what Jody and his family did after he killed the buzzard, and tell what happened to Grandfather. In writing your sequels, begin with a short summary of Steinbeck's plot as the background for your original story. Give your stories new titles.

Themes

As you write your stories, think of issues with which your characters could struggle. Consider these examples.
- Many of Steinbeck's characters struggle with shame and pride. Think about things that make you proud and the kinds of things that would make you ashamed.

- Billy Buck has to decide between saving Nellie and saving the colt. Think about when you have been forced to make a decision between two unpleasant choices. After the red pony dies, Jody realizes that Billy Buck cannot solve all problems. Think about times when you wanted to believe in something even after you knew it probably wasn't true.

Setting

The ranch in *The Red Pony* is based on a ranch that Steinbeck's grandparents' homesteaded near King City, California. Steinbeck sometimes spent his summers there. Salinas, California, the town where Jody was hoping to ride in the rodeo, was Steinbeck's actual home town. Like Steinbeck, you may want to use your own town and neighborhood as the setting for your stories.

Characters

Story characters often reflect experiences and attitudes of the writer. Like Jody in *The Red Pony*, Steinbeck had a pony when he was a child; like Billy Buck, he spent some time working as a ranch hand; and like Grandfather, he liked telling stories. Model your own characters after yourself and people you know.

Visual Images

Steinbeck said that when he wrote he needed to get his mind into the picture-making state. Try to picture the events in your stories. To help you, sketch pictures as you write.

Revising the Draft: Listening to the Sounds of the Story

When revising your stories, choose one or more of the following strategies:
- Once you have a draft, read your story to the class or to small groups. Ask listeners to tell you what they do not understand or how they think the story could be improved. Revise your stories in response to your listeners' comments.

- After Steinbeck wrote his first drafts, he read what he had written into a recording machine. Then he listened to what he had said. When he heard things he didn't like, he revised the story, re-recorded it, and listened to it again. Try reading your draft aloud into a tape recorder. Listen to what you wrote, and revise. Repeat this pattern until you are satisfied with the way your story sounds.

- Have another student read your story aloud to you or to a small group. Listen, as Steinbeck did, for places you want to revise. Ask group members to give suggestions as well.

Illustrating and Publishing the Story Collection

Illustrate your stories. If you are writing an autobiographical collection, illustrate events in your stories by including real photographs if you have them. If you are doing the sequel collection, draw sketches of what you imagine the scenes and characters would look like. Create an attractive cover for your book. Publish your stories by reading them aloud to the class and including them in a class library.

5

ARTISTIC ABILITY

Recent archaeological discoveries in France have uncovered highly sophisticated animal images believed to have been created by cave dwellers 30,000 years ago. Carvings such as these can be found throughout the world, preserving a record of human events long before writing as we know it had been invented. In fact, early writing was itself very pictorial. Manuscripts illustrated ideas with ornate calligraphy and elaborate, brightly colored pictures. Letters in the alphabet, especially the first letter in a section, both adorned the page and, often humorously, summarized the content. Borders on the pages included intricate murals telling stories in even greater detail than the words on the page. Although we think of the practice of picture writing as historical, it is not difficult to see evidence of it continuing in our day. Picture signs are all around us. International driving symbols are just one example.

Like our ancient ancestors, children draw to communicate before they begin to read and write. They express emotions, themes, and ideas through pictures. Because new knowledge comes from observation, activities that ask students to observe the world around them and draw what they see enhance their learning. Visualization marshals imaginative faculties in ways that other forms of expression may not. We usually think of pictures as illustrations of ideas already produced in written text. But pictures can also be the means by which writing ideas are generated. In fact, often the pictures are a major portion, if not all, of the message. *The Mysteries of Harris Burdick* by Chris Van Allsburg, for example—one of the units in this chapter—is a storybook comprised solely of pictures. Readers must provide the words to complete the story.

When language arts teachers encourage multiple forms of artistic expression in the study of literature and writing, they not only generate a rich learning environment for linguistic study, but they also enhance students' appreciation for cultural diversity. Because graphic symbols cut across language and cultural barriers, students see common features in communication systems across time and geography, increasing their understanding both of the power of symbolic language and of the similarities among people. By identifying differences and similarities in communication systems, students gain greater appreciation of the sign systems in other cultures and increased understanding of their own.

Lessons in this chapter ask students both to interpret and to create works of art, as well as to write about what they see. As they reflect in art and writing about their observations and life experiences, they gain greater understanding about the world and their place in it.

John Keats's "Ode on a Grecian Urn" is the focus of the first unit in this chapter. Keats's famous ode was written when he was 23, just three years before his death. He wrote the poem about an ancient vase, a work of fine art. The poem questions the value of youth and the importance of art in culture. The activities ask students to bring in works of art and write about them. They then draw their own picture on a "vase" and write a creative piece in response to their own drawing or to one of the works they brought to class. Students have a chance to discuss their preferences about and responses to artworks and to evaluate their own work.

The Mysteries of Harris Burdick by Chris Van Allsburg is highlighted in the second unit. Van Allsburg's 14 titled and captioned pictures give students an opportunity to collaborate with the author in completing his vision. Students "read" the pictures and then write the narratives that they imagine the fictional writer intended, using the titles, captions, and pictures as interpretive clues. Students also look at features of Van Allsburg's artistic style, and then try to identify features of their personal artistic style and preferences. Finally, like Van Allsburg, they create their own set of titled and captioned pictures for classmates to read and interpret in their own original narratives. Following feedback from classmates, students revise and publish their picture books.

Chinese poems, pictures, and folk tales comprise the final unit in this chapter. Connections between writing and art are particularly apparent in Chinese picture language. In this unit, students read several Chinese folk tales and poems, and they examine two Chinese artworks. In these word and picture stories, students look for evidence of cultural practices and values, both those markedly different from their own, as well as those they find familiar. Students read and write Chinese characters, discovering the underlying logic in these seemingly indecipherable symbols. Finally, they write their own illustrated folk tales, drawing from family and community legends and myths.

Writing With Master Poet John Keats

"Ode on a Grecian Urn"

Composing Strategies Highlighted

1. Writing that grows from looking at art

2. Drawing or sculpting a writing idea

3. Illustrating individual writing

4. Visiting art museums or centers and writing about art

5. Imitating poetic forms

Background Information

John Keats was one of the Romantic poets of England. The Romantics wrote during the 1800s. Their topics included nature, art, the distant past, myths, and common people. Keats lived the shortest life of these poets, dying at age 25 of tuberculosis. Despite his short life, he has often been judged the most talented of the Romantic poets, though poetic status varies with the attitudes of any particular era. Nevertheless, Keats has continued through the past two centuries to be admired and taught across grade levels.

His life began tragically with the early death of his parents, continued with intense work as a medical student and as a writer, and ended in Rome where he had been sent to avoid the English winter. In his short life, however, he wrote many famous and often anthologized poems. Among his most famous are the great odes, "Ode to a Nightingale," "Ode to Autumn," "Ode on Melancholy," and, of course, "Ode on a Grecian Urn."

Keats's great odes were written within a month in April and May of 1819. Shortly after the completion of the odes, his physicians told him to give up writing to protect his failing health. He died two years later in 1821. The poems therefore reflect the passions of a young man facing the knowledge that his talent and life energy were about to end. Each ode treats this tragic theme in its own way.

Keats's odes present profound philosophical questions about the nature of mind, love, symbols, art, beauty, and joy. Cultural critics today might ask whether such abstract and romantic ideals should be the subject of poetry or of art when so many real social questions deserve the attention of artists. In Keats's time, poetry dealt with exactly these abstract issues, and the education of a young man would necessarily have included speculation on abstract ideals. Readers of journals and poetry magazines would have expected to see poems on the topics treated in the odes.

The Grecian urn, itself a product of human art, stimulates abstract questions about what art means to humans who live in a changing world. As long as humans have had consciousness, they have produced some kind of art, as can be noted from prehistoric cave drawings in France. They have also often made their practical items like food dishes and clothing into works of art as well.

The urn pictures two events. One side shows a group of young people playing in the forest, and the other shows a group of people on their way to a religious event. Keats asks whether art in the form of the pictures and the urn itself has more value than the fleeting life of the person who enjoys the art. He asks finally whether human life would have meaning without art and whether art matters when there are no humans. He leaves the reader with the perplexing question.

Students are asked to think about the meaning of visual art. What value does it have for their lives? What art do they enjoy? They have a chance to write about art they admire and to produce their own artwork as a source for composition. Students will enjoy deciding what questions about art and life are important for their generation, nearly two hundred years after Keats wrote his poems.

Getting to Know John Keats's "Ode on a Grecian Urn"

Writing About Art

Imagine holding a beautiful vase in your hands. The vase has pictures on each side. Imagine looking first at one side. On that side some young people are playing in a forest. Some of them have musical instruments, flutes and strings, in their hands. One boy leans over to kiss a girl. He is forever leaning but never kissing. You turn the vase. On the other side a group of villagers lead a young cow up a hillside.

"Ode" means a lyrical poem, one that could possibly be sung. In this case the poet is musing about the pictures he sees on the large vase or urn. The pictures probably looked something like this.

As the poet looks at the vase, he thinks at first that the people on the vase are luckier than we are because they will be forever young. He then thinks, however, that the vase makes us think about our own mortality. He says that when his generation has long gone, the people on the vase will still be the same and their beauty will always be meaningful to humans. He ends by saying that beauty is truth and truth beauty. The ending often strikes readers as sad since Keats was so close to the end of his short life and was working so hard to produce great art in his poems.

People who write and talk about literature have argued about the ending of this poem for many years. Some say that art is more important than anything else in the world. Others say that human values like love and justice are more important than art. Still others say that human life is more important than either art or values. A fourth group argues that all three are dependent on one another. Keats poses the problem in the poem and leaves the reader to think about the answer.

The poem asks whether it would be better to be forever young but never learn from experience or to be alive but face growing older. Our culture seems to put such a high value on youth that we might choose the first point of view.

In a small group discuss how you think the following questions should be answered. Would it be all right to be young forever but always have the same experiences?

Write your ideas below.

_____

_____

_____

_____

_____

_____

How important is art? What kind of art is important to you and your friends?
How should art be supported in our culture? That is, who should pay for it?
How do we decide how much our culture should spend on art and artists?

Talk about these questions with your group. Then write about your reactions to the questions.

_____

_____

_____

_____

_____

_____

_____

_____

_____

_____

_____

Writing About John Keats's "Ode on a Grecian Urn"

Finding Meaning in Art

The "Ode on a Grecian Urn" fits into a class of poetry in which poets talk about artworks. In these poems the poets not only shape a work themselves in the poem, but they also speculate on the meaning of the artwork they are observing. This gives readers a kind of double experience. We can see the poem on the page with its peculiar stanza shapes and rhyme and meter. We can also imagine the artwork being described.

In this case Keats describes a work that is not only beautiful but also very old. He talks about both the look of the vase and the people from long ago who were the models for the artist. Thus readers move from the poem to the imagined vase to ancient Greece itself. Readers' imaginations can roam in several different directions.

1. Find a piece of art that you find beautiful, or at least interesting. If you can, find an interesting object that is both useful and pictorial like the vase. A picture of a museum piece is fine, but something from your own world that you admire is even better. Describe the piece of art.

   _____

   _____

   _____

   _____

   _____

2. Talk about what your artwork means to you in the way that Keats talks about the meaning of the static beauty of the vase. Discuss with your group what "beauty" means to different people. No doubt you all have individual definitions of beauty.

   List several definitions below.

   _____

   _____

   _____

   _____

   _____

3. Keats says to the vase that it only knows about beauty. That's the only truth about life that the vase can give us.

What "truth" about life does your chosen piece of art suggest to you? Write about it.

_____

_____

_____

_____

4. Now find another piece of art. Like the first, it can be a picture, a vase, a sculpture, or even a piece of jewelry. It must, however, be different from the first piece of art that you chose. Describe this piece of art.

_____

_____

_____

_____

5. How is it like the first piece? How is it different? Discuss your chosen artworks with your group. What differences do you see among the pieces of art by members of your group? Talk about what your art says about yourself and your interests.

Write a description of your "taste" in art. What do you like? What don't you like?

_____

_____

_____

_____

_____

_____

_____

Writing With John Keats

Writing About Art

Here is a vase on which you can draw your own art. Think of a picture that you find meaningful. Don't worry as much about artistic ability as the importance of the picture. You might try to imagine what you would find "truthful" in a picture.

Write about the meaning of your picture. Does it relate to your life, to your reading, to your experiences in school, or to other experiences?

_____

_____

_____

Discuss your pictures and your writing with other class members. Ask for ideas about your work. What could you add to your writing to better describe your picture? What do you see in your group members' drawings that interests or surprises you?

Record below your responses to the drawings of your group. Write about your reactions. Whose work was most like yours? Whose work was least like yours? What did you like about other group members' drawings?

_____

_____

_____

Try to write your own "artistic" work either about one of the pieces of art you collected for this unit or about your drawing. Plan a poem, short story, or song.

1.   Write the first lines of the work here:

2.   You may find that you want to move to larger paper or that you want to write on a word processor. You may even use a journal or notebook where you do "creative" writing. This works well for some writers. Below, write a brief sketch of what you plan to write.

3.   Join your group and read the creative work you have written. Talk about your work in relation to your piece of art or drawing. Discuss how each of you in the group used the art as a way to get yourself going on your writing. Below, describe your reactions to this writing activity. Remember that Keats was not very old when he wrote his odes. He was in medical school, so he had other work to do too just as you do. Think about how your creative piece applies to your busy world and to your life.

Writing With Master Storyteller Chris Van Allsburg

The Mysteries of Harris Burdick

Composing Strategies Highlighted

1. Using art as a catalyst for writing

2. Learning to interpret artworks as stories

3. Using art to complete the meaning of a story

4. Comparing revision in art and writing

5. Seeing connections among reading, writing, and art

Background Information

The frame story for the collection of 14 titled and captioned pictures in *The Mysteries of Harris Burdick* is that their fictional creator, Burdick, had written 14 stories, taken key illustrations for each story to a publisher, and then disappeared. Readers must provide their own stories answering the stated or implied questions in the titles and captions.

The Mysteries of Harris Burdick provides an excellent opportunity for students to see that art, like reading, requires the viewer to participate actively in the construction of meaning. Students see art not just as an illustration of a story but as part of the meaning itself. Students often look for the correct meaning in a story, failing to realize that readers actually construct a substantial portion of the story when they bring their own life experiences together with the words on the page to create their interpretations.

Like many students, Van Allsburg loved art activities in the early grades but turned to more popular activities—football in particular—in high school. Not until he went to college did he resume his interest in art. Van Allsburg's art has a number of characteristic features. In fact, although Van Allsburg's frame story in the introduction attributes the pictures to a fictional writer, the work is clearly his own. Van Allsburg's pictures are often described as surrealistic, connecting reality and the world of dreams and the imagination. His stories frequently connect fantastic elements with real people in average circumstances. Board game animals come alive, and pictures with seemingly benign creatures create haunting and chilling moods. Characters' dreams sometimes become the stories, providing plausible backgrounds for fantastic and highly incongruous events. The pictures themselves with their use of light and shadow and skewed lines emphasize the dreamlike quality of the story.

In this unit, students read pictures, creating titles and captions, as well as stories that reflect their interpretations of the pictures. They experiment with strategies for creating mood and distance. They compare strategies for reading and revising both stories and art. Like Van Allsburg, who used pictures in newspapers as catalysts for story ideas, students find stories in their own lives and in the world around them. They draw their own pictures, create titles and captions, and have peers interpret the pictures in original stories. Although students may at first feel intimidated by Van Allsburg's award-winning illustrations, they learn that different artists render their creations in different ways. One activity asks students to reflect on their own art experiences, especially their early drawing and painting, which reflect their uncensored artistic tastes. After writing, sharing, and revising, students publish their "picture books."

Resources

Van Allsburg, Chris. *The Mysteries of Harris Burdick.* Boston: Houghton Mifflin, 1984.

A series of revisions of Georges Seurat's *Sunday Afternoon on the Island of La Grande Jatte* can be found in *Smithsonian* 22.7 (October 1991): 106-09, offering students an excellent opportunity to see revision similarities in art and writing.

Getting to Know Chris Van Allsburg's *The Mysteries of Harris Burdick*

Reading and Writing Picture Stories

When you look at a picture, you naturally connect what you see to experiences you have had. These recollections influence your interpretation of the picture. Depending on the associations generated by the picture, you react emotionally as well. Part of your response is determined by the artist, of course, but some of it comes from your own experiences too. Readers interpret stories the same way, which explains why several people, all reading the same words and all reading carefully, will have different interpretations. Look at the picture below. Because it is an abstract picture—that is, it does not represent specific objects the way they are seen in real life—viewers must use their imagination to create meaning.

Try to imagine yourself as different people viewing this picture. What might you see in it if you were

a scientist? _____

a musician? _____

a writer? _____

an athlete? _____

an artist? _____

Reading Harris Burdick's Pictures

The way you interpret art is similar in many ways to how you interpret a story. Choose one of the pictures from *The Mysteries of Harris Burdick* and answer the questions below. Notice that the questions are similar to questions often asked about works of literature.

Picture Title _____

Caption _____

1. How do you respond emotionally to the picture? Do you see sadness, joy, anger, contemplation, excitement, love, peace, difficulty, danger, or some other emotion in this picture?

   _____

2. Identify what you see (people, objects, shading, lines, etc.).

   _____

   _____

   _____

   _____

3. Describe the situation (What is going on in the picture?).

   _____

   _____

   _____

   _____

   _____

4. Recall an experience that the picture brings to mind. Share your recollections with the class.

   _____

   _____

   _____

   _____

   _____

5. Write a story that you feel fits the title and the caption. Read the stories aloud.

Writing About Chris Van Allsburg's *The Mysteries of Harris Burdick*

Individual Artistic Styles

Just as all people look different and have unique signatures, they write and draw with distinctive styles. Their artistic style is reflected in the subjects they paint, the colors they use, the realism, the shading, the straight or curved lines, and even the types of paint they use. Some artists draw only particular types of people; others draw only mountain or ocean scenes, spotted horses, or blue whales. Some artists always use bright colors which tend to create a cheerful mood. Others use soft colors, which are more likely to create a peaceful mood. Depending on the use of color and line, artists can even make their pictures suggest sound and action.

1. How would you describe Van Allsburg's artistic style?

2. Describe your artistic style. When you draw or paint pictures, what subjects do you tend to choose? What colors? Mood? Are your pictures realistic or abstract? Would you describe them as loud or quiet? Action filled or still? Try to reflect on your early experiences with art—what you liked to create and to view.

Creating Mood With Color

1. Color can create emotional responses in the viewer. For each of these emotions, name what you consider an appropriate color. (The same color may be used more than once.)

sadness	_____	boredom	_____	peace	_____
happiness	_____	love	_____	resentment	_____
anger	_____	hate	_____	jealousy	_____
excitement	_____	humor	_____	fear	_____

2. What word from the list above (or some other word) best describes the tone in each picture?

"Archie Smith, Boy Wonder"_____   "Mr. Linden's Library"_____

"Under the Rug"_____   "The Seven Chairs" _____

"A Strange Day in July"_____   "The Third-Floor Bedroom" _____

"Missing in Venice" _____   "Just Desert"_____

"Another Place, Another Time" _____   "Captain Tory" _____

"Uninvited Guests"_____   "Oscar and Alphonse" _____

"The Harp" _____   "The House on Maple Street" _____

3. Pick a word from the list above and write a journal entry about an important time in your life when you felt this emotion.

4. Using the appropriate colors, draw a picture of this experience. Give your picture a title and a caption.

Creating Mood With Light and Shadow

1. Artists rarely show sun or other light directly in a picture, but the viewer can see the light by the shadows in the picture. Look at the pictures and see whether you can tell where the light is coming from. Working in pairs or small groups, (1) choose two pictures in *The Mysteries of Harris Burdick* that clearly show light and shadows; (2) tell the location of the light source— above right, top left, etc.; and (3) support your answers with examples of objects showing light or shadow. Share your findings with the class and compare your "readings."

Picture Title	Location of Light Source	Light and Shadowed Objects
_____	_____	_____
_____	_____	_____

Using Size, Placement, and Sharpness to Create Distance

2. Artists make objects in a picture appear closer or farther away, depending on the size of the object and where it is placed on the page. Objects that you want to appear farther away need to be placed higher up on the page, and closer objects need to be toward the bottom. Size also is important. Distant objects are smaller and closer objects are larger. Even the sharpness of an object—that is, whether you draw very sharp, distinct lines or give the object a slightly fuzzy appearance—helps to indicate distance. Closer objects are usually more clearly defined, and distant ones are slightly fuzzy. Working in small groups, find one example each of *placement* (an object higher or lower on the page), *size* (larger or smaller than other objects), and *sharpness* (clearness or fuzziness) to reflect the distance of objects in one of the pictures in *The Mysteries of Harris Burdick.* Tell the effect of each.

Placement

Picture Title _____

Object and Effect _____

Size

Picture Title _____

Object and Effect _____

Sharpness

Picture Title _____

Object and Effect _____

Writing With Chris Van Allsburg

Getting Picture Story Ideas From a Newspaper

1. Sometimes Van Allsburg used newspapers to find ideas for his stories and illustrations. Find an unusual story in a newspaper or magazine. Write about the story below.

_____

_____

_____

_____

_____

_____

2. How could you use this newspaper story in a picture story of your own? Write what your story would be about.

_____

_____

_____

3. Draw a picture to suggest your story idea. Try to give it some element of mystery. Give it a title and a caption that requires readers to imagine the story behind it.

Reading Class Pictures

1. Exchange pictures with a classmate. "Read" the picture and write one page telling its story.
2. Share pictures and stories, as well as the artist's story intentions, with one another.
3. On the lines below, identify similarities and differences in the artist's and the reader's interpretations.

Things Unique to Your Story	Things Unique to the Reader's Story	Similarities in Readings
_____	_____	_____
_____	_____	_____
_____	_____	_____
_____	_____	_____
_____	_____	_____

4. Share pictures and interpretations with the class.

Revising Pictures

Like writers, artists revise their paintings—often many times. One famous French artist, Georges Seurat, painted a picture called *Sunday Afternoon on the Island of La Grande Jatte,* which he revised as many as 57 times. This painting began with only grass, trees, water, and a few small boats. Gradually, he added a few people, then animals and more people, young and old, walking, sitting, fishing, boating, and playing until the picture was filled with activity. Like writing a story or an essay, the first draft of a picture usually captures only the general idea. Details come later, and polishing usually comes last.

Revise your picture to use color, light, and shadow to create mood, and use placement, size, and sharpness to show distance. Add details as appropriate. Share draft revisions in small groups or with the class. Revise the pictures in response to the viewers' responses.

Publishing Picture Books

Like Van Allsburg's picture stories, which have generated thousands of different stories, create a class *Mystery* collection that includes both the pictures and the readers' narratives.

Writing With Master Chinese Poets and Storytellers

Stories, Poems, and Pictures From China

Composing Strategies Highlighted

1. Seeing writing as a reflection of culture

2. Visualizing stories

3. Illustrating stories

4. Writing Chinese picture language

5. Writing stories reflecting heritage

Background Information

As schools increasingly become more culturally diverse, students have opportunities to see the traditions, values, and languages of people whose backgrounds differ, often markedly, from their own. The mosaic that emerges from this uniting of cultures is beneficial in many ways. In learning about these groups, students not only broaden their horizons as they learn about others, but they also learn something about themselves as they discover similarities and differences in their backgrounds and cultural practices.

The Asian community, which is growing rapidly in many areas of the country, brings an especially rich heritage for students to study. In many people's minds, China is thoroughly mystical and inaccessible, a belief that derives from a variety of sources. It is indeed geographically remote, and because it is so ancient, it carries on some traditions that seem especially foreign to Westerners. Having only recently opened up after many years of secrecy, China offers intriguing possibilities for students to discover its unique cultural features and, at the same time, to discover common bonds.

The folk tale, poems, and pictures in this unit have been chosen to give students a flavor of old China, whose myths and traditions continue in many ways in modern China. "Three Pools Mirroring the Moon," a Chinese creation myth, explains a destructive cyclone as the work of a giant black fish. Two poems and pictures, "The Silkworm" and "The Painting," show the values and hardships of the peasant class. In several activities, students not only write Chinese characters, but they also discover the underlying logic of the system.

Study of the unit begins with an examination of what the students already know about China. Students are encouraged to do a little research to see what they can add to their knowledge. Like writers everywhere, Chinese poets and storytellers throughout history have used their craft to tell the stories of their lives—their struggles, hopes, values, and dreams. Students conclude their study of this unit by telling their own life stories and those of their ancestors.

Below is a sketch of China with dots indicating the location of some of its most famous cities. Students may enjoy doing a little research to identify the locations and significance of Beijing, Shanghai, Xian, Nanjing, and Hangzhou and to learn more about China's history, geography, and culture. Because Hong Kong will soon be part of China, you may ask them to locate it, too.

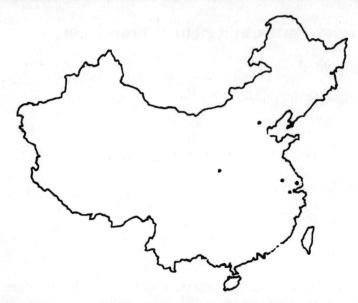

Beijing, in the northeast, has served as the capital of China for many centuries. Tiananmen Square, The Great Hall of the People, the Forbidden City (historical emperors' 250-acre residence, familiar to anyone who has seen the movie *The Last Emperor),* and the nearby Great Wall are a few of the city's most famous landmarks.

Shanghai, located on the coast of the East China Sea, is a large industrial city and major seaport that lays claim to being the most populous city in the world. Because it was under European control for a period of time, it is the most European of Chinese cities, with large sections in which Western architecture dominates. The Yangtzie River flows near Shanghai.

Nanjing, located just north and west of Shanghai, served as the capital of China during several dynasties, most recently under the presidency of Sun Yat-sen. The Yangtzie River (immortalized in the famous children's book, *The Story of Ping)* flows through Nanjing.

Xian, located inland, is the site of one of the most important archaeological finds in the world, with excavations of artifacts that are over 6,000 years old. Excavations have uncovered tombs of emperors and, most important, a spectacular array of 7,000 terra-cotta warriors. The life-size warriors, discovered in 1974, are all lined up as though heading off into battle, some on foot, some on horseback, and some with chariots.

Hangzhou, located just south and west of Shanghai, is considered one of the most beautiful places in China, and is consequently a popular tourist spot. Known particularly for the beauty of scenic West Lake, it is the site of numerous folk tales, which often focus on the historical flooding problems. The story in this unit, "Three Pools Mirroring the Moon," focuses on West Lake at Hangzhou and its destructive storms.

Getting to Know Chinese Folk Tales and Poems

In this unit you will be learning about the ancient Chinese culture through its stories, pictures, poems, and pictorial language. Before reading the following story, make a list of what you already know about China. Make a list on the board of all that the class knows.

Folk tales often explain natural phenomena with gods and goddesses or heroes struggling against evil forces. The following folk tale explains the cause of flooding in the city of Hangzhou, a famous tourist spot on beautiful West Lake. As you read, take notes on words or events that strike you as particularly Chinese.

Three Pools Mirroring the Moon

Once upon a time, Lu Ban and his younger sister, skilled stone carvers of Shandong Province, went to Hangzhou. They rented two rooms by Qiantang Gate and hung out a signboard "The Lus of Shandong, Master Carvers in Stone, Metal and Wood." It said apprentices would be accepted.

Now the house of Lu Ban was well known for carving, and the signboard created a stir in Hangzhou, with young people beating a path to their house to seek apprenticeships. Lu Ban and his sister carefully selected 180 young people to teach the technique of carving. Their skill was such that their carved dogs watched the house, while their wooden cats caught mice. The 180 apprentices all learned to carve equally well.

One day when the Lus were teaching, a dark cyclone whirled through Hangzhou. This was the evil Black Fish Spirit coming to scourge the earth. The Black Fish Spirit dived into the middle of West Lake, digging down 4,000 feet and taking up permanent residence there. The whole city of Hangzhou was polluted with the stench when the Black Fish Spirit breathed. And when it spat in the pool, the foothills of north and south mountains were submerged. The willows along West Lake shores cracked, flowers rotted. West Lake was so filled with foul water that it overflowed and polluted the entire beautiful city of Hangzhou.

Lu Ban and his sister and their 180 apprentices climbed Precious Stone Mountain and saw the distressed people fleeing the stinking flood around West Lake. In the middle of the lake they saw a monstrous fish mouth spewing out foul air and dirty dark water. The giant fish mouth rose gradually out of the water, until the whole head thrust skyward. Then suddenly the Black Fish Spirit leapt onto a dark cloud and disappeared in the sky. The same dark cloud hovered over the lake, then floated towards Precious Stone Mountain, where it settled, and from out of it emerged a very ugly fat man. He approached Lu Ban's sister, leering at her with bulging eyes.

"What work do you do, my charming young lady?" he asked. "I'm a master craftsman," she replied. The disgusting man inspected Sister Lu from head to foot and said, "But you have such bright eyes and curved eyebrows, you must be good at sewing. Come with me and make me some new clothes." Sister Lu flatly refused. Again he looked the young woman up and down. "And you're so slim, with such slender fingers, you must be skilled in embroidering the dragon and phoenix. Come along, embroider a satin quilt for me." Sister Lu stood mute. The ugly creature then grabbed Sister Lu by the arm. "My lovely young maiden, I don't care if you can neither sew nor embroider. Marry me and you'll have the best food and clothes. You'll have a comfortable and easy life."

Lu Ban appeared and loosened the creature's grip on his sister with a sledge hammer. "Get out!" he shouted. But the creature sneered: "My skin is three feet thick and I'm not afraid of your hammer. If your sister marries me, I'll treat you well. If not, the city will be flooded and the people drowned." Sister Lu thought that would be a terrible catastrophe for the people of Hangzhou, and she said, "I'll marry you after my brother prepares the dowry."

Overjoyed, the creature promised to wait. "But what dowry do you want?" he asked. "A stone incense burner carved by my brother out of cliffs," Sister Lu answered. "Fine, fine, fine," exclaimed the creature clapping his hands. "The Black Fish King will come to earth to build a temple. The gift of your stone incense burner will be just the thing for collecting donations."

Sister Lu had a talk with her brother, then Lu Ban told the ugly creature, "But water surrounds us on both sides. You must make the water subside before I can start carving." The ugly creature opened his huge mouth and sucked in the flood in one breath. The refugees in the mountains could now go to their homes. Lu Ban next pointed to a steep crag and said to the ugly creature, "How about splitting that crag so I can carve the incense burner from half of it?" The creature applauded the idea. "Great! Hurry, and the bigger the better."

"But could you move it if it was so big?" pursued Lu Ban. The ugly creature laughed, "I only have to lift one foot to cause a cyclone that will easily move a mountain. A tiny incense burner is nothing." With that he was carried up by the cyclone.

Lu Ban, Sister Lu and the 180 apprentices climbed Precious Stone Mountain, where Lu Ban rolled up his sleeves, lifted his sledge hammer and came down with it with all his might. Time and again their hammers fell, and after 182 strokes the crag split from top to bottom with a roar like thunder. Half of Precious Stone Mountain lay on the ground, while the other half stood as a precipice. The half on the ground was so big that they wondered how they could carve it. Then Lu Ban, from the center of the rock, estimated the depth of West Lake at its deepest part by measuring it with a very long rope. Then Lu Ban handed the other end of the rope to his sister, who made one round of the rock.

Having made a rough outline of the size of the carving all set to work chipping out the stone burner, their chisels on the rock filling the ravine with sound. After 49 days a very, very large incense burner had been carved out of the crag. Yet they went on carving, decorating the legs like three inverted gourds, each with three window-like holes for light to go through. When all was completed, the ugly creature appeared at the foot of Precious Stone Mountain with a bridal sedan chair and procession beating drums and blowing trumpets. He had come for the bride.

"Move the dowry to your place first," said Lu Ban. "My sister is preparing." The ugly creature, overjoyed at the prospect of having the lovely maiden as his own, ran home as fast as he could, a cyclone behind him carrying the stone incense burner along after him. Reaching the middle of West Lake he turned into a big black fish and dived into the depths. The incense burner following him turned over and came to rest snugly over the bottom of West Lake. The Black Fish Spirit tried to stir up a cyclone under the stone incense burner but there was not enough room. All he could do was to dig deeper down into the lake. The stone incense burner was sucked down firmer and firmer in the lake, and the people of Hangzhou knew that the Lus had defeated the Black Fish Spirit and all went to the lake to celebrate the victory. Finally the Black Fish Spirit died of suffocation under the stone incense burner, which remained fixed with only its three gourd-shaped carved legs showing above the water.

That evening, Lu Ban and Sister Lu and the people of Hangzhou went out on West Lake by boat and placed lighted candles in the hollowed out legs of the incense burner. They sang and danced all the night through, happy to have their city and its lake lovely and clean again. Fishing boats plied the lake as before, flowers and trees flourished on its banks. West Lake became even more beautiful. Now on West Lake on each Mid-Autumn Festival eve, people light candles and place them inside the lanterns made in the legs of that giant incense burner, their light shining through the openings and reflecting on the water like three small moons, while the harvest moon is reflected in the center of the lake. People call this spot in West Lake, "The Three Pools Mirroring the Moon."

1. Working in pairs or small groups, make a list of words or ideas that seem to you to reflect the Chinese culture.

2. Select one scene to illustrate.

3. Rewrite a shortened version of the story to reflect American culture rather than Chinese culture. Read your stories aloud in class and discuss what you learned about differences in the cultures.

4. This story of the Black Fish Spirit is intended to explain the activity of a cyclone (also known as a tornado). Make up your own folk tale explaining some natural phenomena (lightning, thunder, stars, drought, wind) or telling why birds have wings, giraffes have long necks, elephants have tusks, etc. Illustrate your story.

Name _____

Appreciating Cultural Differences: Reading and Responding to Pictures

Many of the questions that active readers ask about stories, they also ask about pictures. Study the pictures below that reflect the culture of China. Answer the questions about each.

1. How do you feel when you see the picture?

   _____

2. Identify what you see (people, objects, etc.).

   _____

   _____

3. Describe the situation. What is going on?

   _____

   _____

4. What experience does the picture call to mind?

   _____

   _____

5. Give the picture a title.

   _____

Answer the same questions about this picture.
1. How do you feel when you see this picture?

   _____

2. Identify what you see (people, objects, etc.).

   _____

   _____

3. Describe the situation. What is going on?

   _____

   _____

4. What experience does the picture call to mind?

   _____

   _____

5. Give the picture a title.

   _____

   _____

Writing About Chinese Poems and Folk Tales

Below are the poems whose illustrations you saw on page 99. Answer the questions to the right of each poem. Compare your responses with your readings of the pictures.

An Old Painting

Zhao Dian (c. 1650)

I have an old painting at home;
It is worth a couple of cities.
I could not bear to exchange it for rice from the street
So I returned with a pot filled with snow.

古　画

明末·赵　甸

吾家有古画，

其价重连城。

不易街头米，

归来雪满罂。

1. What does the writer/culture appear to value?

   _____
   _____
   _____

2. How are these values similar to or different from your own or your community's values?

   _____
   _____
   _____
   _____
   _____
   _____

A Woman Raising Silkworms

Zhang Yu (c. 1170)

Yesterday she went into town,
Returning she drenched her handkerchief with tears.
Of all those who dress themselves in silk
There is no one who raises silkworms.

蚕　妇

宋·张　俞

昨日入城市，

归来泪满巾。

遍身罗绮者，

不是养蚕人。

1. What does the writer/culture appear to value?

   _____
   _____

2. How are these values similar to or different from your own or your community's values?

   _____
   _____
   _____
   _____
   _____
   _____

Writing With Chinese Storytellers

Although Chinese characters look very different from English letters and numbers, they follow logical patterns. See whether you can see the logic in the numbers and words below.

Numbers and Money

In the middle column below are the Chinese characters corresponding to the Arabic numerals in the left column. In the right-hand column, try writing some Chinese numbers.

		Write the following numbers in Chinese characters:
1, 2, 3, 4, 5	一二三四五	3 _____
6, 7, 8, 9, 10	六七八九十	10 _____
20, 30, 40	二十，三十，四十	30 _____ 7 _____
50, 60, 70	五十，六十，七十	70 _____
80, 90, 100	八十，九十，一百	
101, 102	一百零一，一百零二	Can you supply the missing characters to make the number 105?
103, 104	一百零三，一百零四	_____ 百零 _____

The Chinese characters below represent amounts of money. The first character in the pair is the symbol for the *number,* and the second character is the symbol for the word *cents.* Using the information above, fill in the blanks so that the amounts of money are written below in both the Chinese and English languages.

Chinese	English	Chinese	English	Chinese	English
三分	_____	_____	4 cents	_____	8 cents
五分	_____	_____	7 cents	_____	7 cents
十分	_____	_____	9 cents	_____	2 cents

Days of the Week and Months of the Year

Look at some characters that identify the days of the week and the months of the year. See whether you can figure out how to write the missing characters.

Monday	星期一	Thursday	星期 _____	January	一月	April	_____ 月	July	_____
Tuesday	星期二	Friday	星期 _____	February	二月	May	_____ 月	August	_____
Wednesday	星期 _____	Saturday	星期 _____	March	_____ 月	June	_____ 月	September	_____

Culture and Language

As you have seen, Chinese writing is very pictorial, sometimes suggesting the meaning of words. Do these characters suggest the meaning in any way to you?

入口 entrance   出口 exit   人 person

Because it would be difficult to pronounce the sounds of the picture characters, China also has a spoken language called *Pinyin* that uses the same letters that we use. The next time you go into a Chinese restaurant, you may want to say "Hello" when you arrive, "Thank you" when you receive your food, and "Good-bye" when you leave. Practice using these words in class.

ni hao	(pronounced *nee how* in English)	means hello
xie xie	(pronounced *shay shay* in English)	means thank you
zaijian	(pronounced *zi-jen* in English)	means good-bye

Writing Folk Tales and Family Legends

For your final project, write a folk tale or family legend. Your story can be entirely true, partly fictional, or completely fictional. Before you begin writing, do some work to generate ideas.

1. Recall a story told by an older family member—especially a story that is told over and over again. If your family members immigrated to this country, tell any stories you know about their experiences. Interview family members, asking them to offer additional details and related stories. Write a journal entry about these experiences. Share the stories with the class. As classmates tell their stories, take notes when you recall similar details of your own family legends.

2. Tell about a memorable incident from your own life. Childhood recollections are especially good for providing vivid detail. Write a journal entry about this experience and share it with the class. If classmates' stories remind you of similar experiences of your own, write them down.

3. Write about your community. What values and traditions are important? What are the people like? Describe the kinds of work they do; the kinds of entertainment they have—parks, theaters, sports fields, etc.; and their celebrations. Based on the appearance and activities of the town, tell what you think community members consider important.

4. From all of this material, write the first draft of a story about your family, about your community, about yourself, or about all three. Or, if you prefer, write a folk tale incorporating material from the writing you have done here, as well as the folk tale that you began on page 98. Illustrate your story.

5. Share finished stories in small groups. Get feedback from classmates and revise.

6. Read the final drafts aloud to the class. Bind the completed stories in a book.

SCIENTIFIC AND MATHEMATICAL ABILITY

The history of logic, numerical reasoning, and scientific investigation often has more honor than interest attached to it. At least some students find these areas intimidating. Others, of course, find these areas the best part of life. It can be fun to find out about how various kinds of measures began. A foot, for instance, really was the length of a man's foot. Of course, that meant that different people measured a foot differently. A horse's height is measured in hands. At one time the "hand" really was a man's hand. Now it is four inches, as a foot is twelve. English measures have their origins in such humble beginnings as those described above, measurements that worked quite well until the introduction of modern technology. Rockets just will not fire if their components are measured in the length of some part of a person's body, nor will computer chips work in various computers if the size and shape are not uniform.

The history of scientific learning is equally fascinating. What is "true" in science changes from century to century. At one time, of course, scientists saw the earth as the center of the observable universe, which, of course, it was before modern telescope, rockets, and satellites. Today, much more of the universe is observable. The minute observations, as well as the distant observations, have changed considerably. Some scientists think today that genetic engineering will be as revolutionary in the next few years as the change in the supposed center of the universe was in the sixteenth century. Scientific learning continues to change like a giant mystery novel.

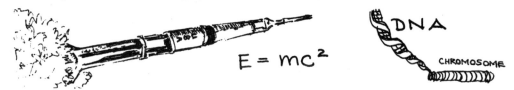

$$E = mc^2$$

DNA

CHROMOSOME

The units in this section will invite students to work together in groups to create and solve problems reflecting issues and events that occur not only in the real world at large, but in their own lives. Students articulate and analyze problems in journal entries, in investigative reports, and in creative narratives. As with other units, students use their own experiences to discover research questions, and throughout the projects, they are asked to reflect on their learning.

Throughout this book, emphasis has been placed on ways of knowing in various disciplines. By having students look at the world through the various lenses of sports, music, art, and science, they see that all subject areas have unique perspectives and each discipline has its own questions and its own procedures for helping people acquire new knowledge. By looking at these multiple ways of knowing, students expand their understanding, not only of individual subject areas, but of knowledge itself.

Avi's *The Blue Heron is* the focus of the first unit. In this novel Maggie, the main character, studies a blue heron while she visits her father and stepmother. At one point in the story, she wants to be exactly like the blue heron. Like Avi's main character, students study an animal which interests them. Using this animal's charateristics and habits, based on actual observation as well as knowledge gained through library research, students write their own stories.

The second unit looks at Ursula Le Guin's *A Wizard of Earthsea*. This story deals with the development of a master wizard in a world where scientific principles also apply to telekinetic and telepathic activities. Students work with scientific inquiry, especially asking moral and ethical questions about medical and technological research. They then do their own anthropological study of a piece of land or community with the opportunity to interview experts and write up their findings in a scientific report.

Madeleine L'Engle's *The Arm of the Starfish* is the final selection in this chapter. Students examine the scientific basis for the book—the regenerative abilities of starfish. In her book L'Engle extends these regenerative properties to other animals and even to humans. Students apply some of the same composing strategies used by L'Engle to their own writing. They also examine settings, characters, and the conflict of good versus evil—elements that L'Engle skillfully weaves into her plot. They finally create their own science fiction stories, starting with a scientific principle and expanding that concept to the world of science fiction by developing "what if" scenarios. A classroom anthology of science fiction stories results.

Writing With Master Novelist Avi

Blue Heron

Composing Strategies Highlighted

1. Observing wildlife to create a story

2. Creating believable characters

3. Focusing on character relationships

4. Using logical deduction to solve problems

Background Information

Most readers know Avi for his historical fiction; however, he also writes mysteries, adventures, fantasies, and realistic novels, both serious and humorous. Avi remembers always liking to read, and he comes from a family of writers. His great grandparents, one grandmother, both parents, and his twin sister all wrote.

Dysgraphia, a brain disorder that causes a person to reverse letters and misspell words when writing, brought Avi much trouble in school. Teachers viewed him as sloppy and found he had difficulty in paying attention. These impairments kept Avi from getting good grades, yet he continued to write despite receiving papers covered in red ink. He says that he did not pay too much attention to those papers or their corrections but saved them—only to write more and more. For this reason Avi serves as an excellent model for students who do not do well with traditional school assignments. By reading Avi's works and by studying his composing strategies, students learn they can overcome certain limiting obstacles and still become successful writers.

Avi credits a playwriting class he took in college for getting him to write seriously. In this class the instructor gave him specific instructions on how to write, even supplying charts for organizing thoughts and events. When Avi began writing for publication, he started by writing down stories he had previously told to his sons. Although his sons eventually outgrew storytelling, Avi continued to write for young adults.

Avi's method of drafting closely follows the logical/mathematical/scientific mode of thinking which shows the ability to notice logical patterns and to follow or generate long chains of reasoning. He begins with ideas and then outlines (in his head as much as on paper) the events of the story, keeping them to 20 or fewer. He spends much time on this concise outline, making numerous revisions while continually focusing on events. Avi feels that the first few paragraphs of any work are important because young adult readers do not allow an author much time to capture their interest. As Avi drafts, he rereads and rewrites, responding as a listener, often rewriting up to 15 drafts. Consequently, his composing strategy amounts to a quick first draft followed by slow, tedious rewrites.

Although Avi would probably not consider himself a mathematician or a scientist, his composing methods closely follow the logical minds of people working in these areas. The activities in this unit use Avi's *Blue Heron* to encourage students to study an animal. Students are also encouraged to focus on logical thinking patterns, using graphic organizers to keep events, character relationships, and their thoughts in order so that they can focus on them and incorporate them into stories.

Getting to Know Avi's *Blue Heron*

Scientific Observation

Maggie studies the blue heron every day. At one point she decides she wants to be the blue heron. Reread the parts of the book which tell about what Maggie notices as she watches the bird and what she learns from her observations of it. Write your notes after the appropriate chapter numbers.

Chapter 5 _____

_____

_____

Chapter 7 _____

_____

_____

Chapter 10 _____

_____

_____

Chapter 29 _____

_____

_____

Again using her powers of acute observation, Maggie acquires much information about Tucker before she meets him. Reread Chapter 11 and list those things Maggie uses to create a picture of Tucker's personality.

_____   _____

_____   _____

_____   _____

_____   _____

Making Logical Connections

Although we do not usually associate magic with scientific principles, Avi uses a logical progression in reference to Maggie's attitude toward magic. Reread the parts of the book in which Avi incorporates magic. Write your notes after the appropriate chapters. As you reread the chapters, think about the following question: What is magic?

Chapter 1 _____

_____

Chapter 14 (end) _____

_____

Chapter 22_____

_____

Chapter 25 (beginning) _____

_____

Chapter 29_____

_____

In small groups share your findings. Discuss Mr. Lavchek's remark to Maggie that magic does not work. Do group members agree or disagree?

Using your notes, any other evidence from the book, and your group discussion, write one or more paragraphs demonstrating how Maggie views magic throughout the book. Include in your response the ways magic helps Maggie through some difficult times.

Writing About Avi's *Blue Heron*

Defining and Classifying

In Chapter 7 Mr. Lavchek defines the word *omen* and proceeds to tell Maggie that the heron is considered an omen for either *life* or *death*. Complete the following:

- Using Chapter 7, define *omen.*

In Chapter 26 Maggie wonders whether her father's problems occurred because she watched the heron. Later she fears that if something happens to the heron, her father will die. She then decides that if she can touch the heron, everything will be okay.

- Considering Maggie's thoughts, do you feel the heron is an omen for life or an omen for death? Why? Write a paragraph classifying the heron as one or the other. Be certain to support your decision with details from the novel.

Comparing and Contrasting

As Maggie studies Tucker in Chapter 19, she remembers how mystery stories always seem to work the same way. Choose one of the following:

- Using evidence from Chapter 19, compare and contrast mystery stories and real life.

- Using evidence from Chapter 19, compare and contrast villains found in stories with Tucker.

Persuading

Because they get the facts first, scientists and mathematicians (logical thinkers) are usually good at the art of persuasion. Gather the facts and then write one of the following persuasive letters:

- Write a letter from Maggie to her father persuading him to take his medicine. List reasons for him to take it.

- Write a letter from Mrs. Lavchek to Mr. Lavchek persuading him to spend more time with the baby. List the benefits of developing that relationship.

- Write a letter from Maggie to Tucker persuading him not to shoot the heron.

Analyzing Relationships

Twelve-year-old Maggie learns a lot about her father and her stepmother during her stay at Sawdy Pond. She also learns a lot about her father and stepmother's relationship during the month, which causes her to think about her relationship with each of them. Select one of the following relationships: Maggie and her father, Maggie and her stepmother, and Maggie's father and stepmother. Use the chart below to identify each character's traits and attitudes toward the other character. Place key words about their relationship in the empty spaces.

Character _____	Character _____
likes and dislikes	likes and dislikes
problems	problems
personality	personality
attitude toward other character	attitude toward other character

On a separate sheet of paper, describe this relationship using key words and phrases from your chart. Be certain to include how the relationship evolves during the course of the novel. Include your advice on how these two characters can improve their relationship.

Writing With Avi

Creating Stories From Observations

In chapter 8, Maggie decides to be like the heron. What animal would you like to be? Like Maggie, choose some animal that has qualities that you think you would like as a symbol of yourself. Observe this animal at least four times, preferably at different times on different days. Use the following to help you.

Name of animal _____

Scientific classification _____

Observation time and date_____

Physical description _____

_____

_____

Behaviors _____

_____

_____

Eating habits _____

How long observed _____

On another sheet of paper, do a science report on your chosen animal, including library research as well as notes based on your own personal observations.

Write a story about your animal. In *Blue Heron* Mr. Lavchek says that the heron can mean life or death. Like Avi you may want the animal to become a symbol of a character, of a theme, or of an event in your story.

Reseeing and Revising the Story

Avi begins his novels with a quick outline (often in his head) and then spends much time slowly revising his work, responding to it as a listener. Because the first few paragraphs of a story must quickly grab readers' attention, he considers introductions extremely important. Reseeing and revising his work consumes much of Avi's time; in fact, 15 rewrites are not an unusual number for him. Like Avi, "resee" your work.

1. Ask a partner to listen to your story.

2. Read it to your partner.

3. Ask your partner for suggestions. You and your partner may consider the following:
   • the introduction
   • the description of the animal
   • the sequence of events—is it logical?
   • the characters—are they believable?
   • the ending

4. List two of those suggestions below.

Area to improve _____
Rewrite:

Area to improve _____
Rewrite:

Writing with Master Storyteller Ursula Le Guin

A Wizard of Earthsea

Composing Strategies Highlighted

1. Writing to understand the natural world

2. Using scientific knowledge to write

3. Drawing maps of the natural world

4. Writing about classifications

5. Doing research with a team

Background Information

A mild and modest person, Ursula Le Guin constructs stories in the peaceful quiet of her northern Pacific home. She is the child of a scientist herself and has a keen interest in all sorts of scientific research, but she tends to like creating her own science so that her readers can look with a new vision on the accepted truth of current scientific investigation as we know it.

Science for Le Guin includes psychology and sociology as well as biology, geography, meteorology, chemistry, physics, and metaphysics. She considers the world of the magical and mystical a scientific arena similar to the world we can perceive through the senses and measure numerically. Thus her novels play with personal and social questions as well as with theories about the structure of the natural and supernatural world.

In the first volume of the Earthsea trilogy, Le Guin speculates on a world in which magic is a scientific reality that operates by sensible and measurable rules in the same way that gravity and laws of motion and thermodynamics operate.

A Wizard of Earthsea investigates the intersections between philosophical, psychological, and scientific knowledge. In this novel a young boy comes to self-knowledge. Le Guin traces his growing awareness of the truth that the "reality that counts is the one which we see when we close our eyes." The main character, Ged, has to learn that the scientific truths of his world can be discovered and mastered only after he has harnessed his own impulses.

Le Guin wrote the novel in the aftermath of the discovery of atomic energy with all attendant terrors and promises. She took the mood of the day into account in making the main character, Ged, a magician/scientist in training. He discovers that if he uses dangerous scientific knowledge too quickly, he will cause both himself and those around him a great deal of trouble.

Ursula Le Guin might not classify herself as a science fiction writer, though her work certainly looks at the world from various imagined scientific points of view. She has investigated the possibilities of other worlds in which gender differences and color differences do not exist. She has also speculated on worlds in which girls have heroic adventures similar to those of boys. Whatever way we "classify" her work, she certainly challenges traditional thinking about the natural and political world we inhabit.

The activities in this unit help students work through scientific research projects to discover for themselves in their writing and in their discussions the responsibilities they have as discoverers of knowledge. They must deal with moral dilemmas that ask them to question the value of scientific knowledge and its various uses. They also have a chance to discuss and discover ways in which they can be socially responsible discoverers of their world.

Students write about their own views of science and discovery and have a chance to exchange those views with classmates. They then have the opportunity to investigate their views through research projects that involve field research. The activities will demand some footwork in their towns or neighborhoods as well as scientific observation of their discoveries and careful recording of those observations.

Getting to Know Ursula Le Guin's *A Wizard of Earthsea*

Writing About Science

"Science" means knowledge. Just as there are many kinds of knowledge, there are also many kinds of science. The ways of knowing about and discovering the world include such activities as measuring, counting, weighing, observing, and analyzing various objects and events. The physical scientists look at objects in the world to discover what these objects are and do. Social scientists look at human, and sometimes animal, psychology and political structure to see how they operate in our world.

In *A Wizard of Earthsea,* Le Guin introduces a world in which science (knowledge) includes what psychologists in this world call telekineses (moving objects and forces with mental power) and telepathy (communicating mentally). The "science" in Earthsea works through the power of words, especially naming. The task of the young hero, called Duny, Sparrowhawk, and Ged as he goes through various stages of development, is to learn first the true names of things in the world in order to control them. Later, he learns how natural forces, like weather and gravity, can also be controlled through mental concentration.

The problem the hero faces is a psychological one. He is headstrong and proud, unable to follow the lead of older and wiser teachers. His pride brings him to use his powers in dangerous ways and almost leads to his own destruction. The novel asks the reader to speculate on the dangers of intellectual pride in knowledge. The reader has to consider what knowledge is good and how it should be used.

Le Guin wrote *A Wizard of Earthsea* during the Vietnam War at the height of the nuclear arms race. She certainly questioned the value of producing nuclear weapons with scientific knowledge and the value of using other weapons in war. She seems to ask whether it was a responsible use of knowledge to use its applications in destructive ways.

Modern psychology and psychiatry investigate how humans use their mental powers for both good and evil. In the story Ged tries to apply his knowledge of magical spells to a task that is far beyond his abilities. In doing so he releases a frightful creature into his world that he must pursue and capture. He finally discovers that the creature is really a part of himself. Psychology speculates that much of what we fear in the world is really a part of our own makeup. Sociologists also suggest that groups and nations get into fights because they tend to see their own worst characteristics in someone else.

Ged cannot become a great person until he has discovered that he must control his own dark side, in the same way that Luke Skywalker makes that discovery in the *Star Wars* movies.

Discuss with your group something about scientific discoveries that you find important. How can they be used for good?

List some possibilities below.

_____
_____
_____
_____
_____
_____

Now think about how scientific knowledge has been used for bad ends in human history. Talk about this idea with your group. In the rest of this section, you will be investigating the ways that people use science.

Writing About Ursula Le Guin's *A Wizard of Earthsea*

Discovery and Analysis

Early in the novel Ged meets his teacher, Ogion. Ogion is a healall, a physician who heals by magic. He teaches Ged his great magic after healing him from his first overuse of magical powers. Ged learns his science of magic by following his teacher in the day-to-day activities of a healall. In most science, especially in medicine, a young apprentice learns from an expert. At research universities and medical schools, young scientists and interns sign on with established researchers and work on projects already in progress. This apprentice system dates back to earliest human history.

The story of the intern who oversteps his or her abilities is as familiar as the wizard's apprentice in Disney's *Fantasia* or as recent as the latest television medical show. Today medical scientists deal with technology and drugs far more powerful than ever before in history so that the possibilities for cure and the possibilities for error have grown.

1. Talk with an older relative or find a medical book from fifty or so years ago. How were diseases treated in the past? How were teeth replaced, for instance? How long did people stay in the hospital after surgery or the delivery of babies? Compare medicine as you know it now with what older people recall. Write about your discoveries.

_____

_____

_____

_____

_____

_____

_____

_____

_____

_____

_____

_____

_____

2. Medical science has moved into areas of ethical debates. Since technology has become so advanced and so expensive, people argue about who should get which medical treatment.

   Dicuss with your group a medical dilemma such as who should get an available heart or kidney replacement—a healthy young person or a wise elderly doctor who could cure others. Think of other dilemmas such as this one and list them below.

   _____
   _____
   _____
   _____
   _____
   _____
   _____

3. Medical technology becomes even more complex when it can be used to produce dangerous weapons. People do not talk about nuclear weapons very much anymore, not nearly as much as they did when Le Guin was writing this novel. They do talk about how bacteria, viruses, and poisoned substances can be used to terrorize civilians and win conflicts between nations.

   What responsibilities do scientists (the wizards of our time) have for their research into dangerous substances? Should they do such research? If they do, who controls it—individuals, private companies, or governments?

   Discuss these questions with your group and summarize your conclusions below.

   _____
   _____
   _____
   _____
   _____
   _____
   _____
   _____
   _____
   _____

Writing with Ursula Le Guin

Writing About Science

Science writing can follow many different paths. You may already have specific interests in scientific areas, but the following activities will give you a few new scientific directions in which to go. For this project you will need a notebook, pen, colored pencils, and some walking shoes.

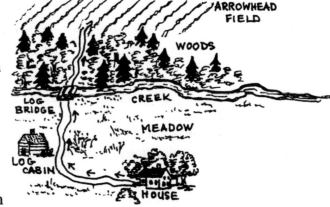

1. With a co-investigator (another member of your group), pick a place that you would like to investigate. It may be a field or farm such as the place that Duny/Ged first herds goats in his youth, or it may be a block in a town or city. You will need your notebook and writing materials.

   Take a walking tour of your area. Write down what you see and draw a map of the area. You might want to divide the writing and drawing responsibilities, or you might both want to keep a record.

2. After you have drawn your map and written down your observations of the area, carry your notebook back to the area. If it is a field in the country, find local people to ask about the area. If it is in town, ask people who live there or work in the area.

   Ask the following questions or others you develop:

   Who has owned the land or buildings?
   When was the area settled?
   What has it been used for?
   What kinds of things are planted?
   What kinds of animals or businesses occupy the land?

3. Consult with your co-investigator about the meaning of your research findings. Write a summary of your findings.

_____

_____

_____

_____

_____

_____

4. Imagine that you are an anthropologist (a scientist who studies different societies). What sorts of conclusions would you come to about the area you investigated? What does your information tell you about the area you investigated? Do you and your co-investigator agree on your findings?

Write your conclusions below.

_____

_____

_____

_____

_____

_____

_____

5. What have you discovered about yourself as a discoverer of knowledge? What responsibilities do you have when investigating the world? What should you do with your new information? Is there a way that you can use it to improve the world? If not, what have you learned about the process of investigation?

_____

_____

_____

_____

_____

_____

_____

_____

_____

Writing With Master Novelist Madeleine L'Engle

The Arm of the Starfish

Composing Strategies Highlighted

1. Focusing on setting

2. Examining plots for the genre of science fiction

3. Analyzing conflict

4. Reusing a character

5. Writing a science fiction story

Background Information

For many middle school students the attraction of science fiction is a strong one. Even reluctant readers seem to enjoy the excitement and possibilities the genre offers as they vicariously embark on fantastic adventures. Books by Madeleine L'Engle provide young readers many such adventures. Although L'Engle is most well known for *A Wrinkle in Time*, the first science fiction novel to firmly establish itself in the field of young adult literature, she has written nearly 40 other books, many of them science fiction or fantasy.

L'Engle is another example of an author who, as a student, did not do well in the traditional school setting. An illness acquired when L'Engle was three caused one leg to be shorter than the other. She was not too social and limped when tired, two characteristics which caused her problems at school. To L'Engle it appeared that teachers equated athletic ability with intelligence and, consequently, she became accustomed to doing poorly in school. Rather than trying to do better athletically, she went home and dreamed and wrote; she also became an avid reader. Yet these skills did not carry over to school. In fact, once when she won a poetry contest, a teacher accused her of copying the winning poem. L'Engle's mother brought a lot of Madeleine's writing to school to convince the teacher that Madeleine did, indeed, write that poem. Eventually L'Engle became a successful student. At Smith College, under the guidance of enthusiastic English professors, she continued to write and graduated with honors. Not only did L'Engle prove herself to be a successful student, she also proved herself to be an extremely successful writer of science fiction and fantasy for young adults.

From reading her books it would appear that scientific principles would come naturally to L'Engle. But a vivid memory she has is that of blowing up the chemistry lab as a student. Her possibly limited natural abilities in the area of science did not prevent her from writing science fiction stories. She read and studied, learning what she needed to know for her stories. She used her knowledge of Einstein's theory of relativity and Max Karl E. L. Planck's quantum theory as the basis for *A Wrinkle in Time*. Because the main characters in *A Wind in the Door* travel into the world of mitochondria, she purchased textbooks to study mitochondria. Studying gave her the knowledge necessary to establish a scientifically accurate foundation to make travel into space and into the minute world of mitochondria believable to readers. However, the use of scientific knowledge as the background for her stories did not make L'Engle an immediate success in the genre of science fiction. She experienced difficulty getting her first science fiction/fantasy book published—twenty-six publishers turned down *A Wrinkle in Time*.

L'Engle usually begins writing with the five senses, then concentrates on her imagination. She writes and then reads the first pages to her family. When writing *The Arm of the Starfish*, L'Engle would compose during the morning and read what she had written to her mother and her son later during that same day. Once her son asked her to change the part where Joshua dies; he could not understand why L'Engle, as the author, had to make a good character die. Her husband also reads her manuscripts, going over each very carefully, cutting and tightening. After reading *The Arm of the Starfish*, he advised her to tighten the plot, a criticism which led L'Engle to rewrite the last third of the novel extensively.

In *The Arm of the Starfish* Adam Eddington goes to the island of Gaea, which lies off the coast of Portugal, to work on the regenerative properties of starfish with Dr. O'Keefe. Dr. O'Keefe has extended his experiments to other animals and even humans. In keeping within the parameters of science fiction, L'Engle bases the plot on a real scientific principle, regeneration. She then asks the question, "What if the same principle could be applied to humans?" The plot unfolds quickly as Adam learns that two groups are fighting for control of the findings of the research. Much to Adam's consternation, he cannot distinguish the good group from the bad group.

In this unit students examine L'Engle's composing strategies as well as the genre of science fiction. They are encouraged to explore scientific concepts before they write their own stories. They focus on settings, base plots on scientific principles, work with "what if" scenarios, and then write their own science fiction stories.

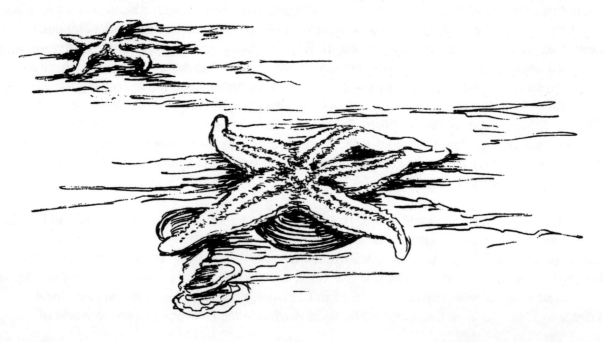

Getting to Know Madeleine L'Engle's *The Arm of the Starfish*

Establishing the Setting

The Arm of the Starfish takes place in several settings. Each place has a hint of the exotic and a bit of mystery in it. Settings include Kennedy International Airport, Madrid, the island of Gaea, and Lisbon. On another sheet of paper, describe each of these settings. After each description, include the senses upon which L'Engle relies to establish the place.

Borrowing From Poetry

L'Engle uses lines from Robert Frost's poem, "Two Tramps in Mud Time," as a password. In what ways does the meaning of Frost's lines fit the theme of the book?

_____

_____

_____

_____

Finding Characters in Previous Works

Calvin O'Keefe appears in L'Engle's Time Science Fantasy series, and Adam Eddington appears in the later book, *A Ring of Endless Light*. In fact, L'Engle frequently revives characters from previous works with much success. How does this composing strategy affect the later story? When an author reuses a character in a later work, what must he or she remember to do?

Inventing New Characters

L'Engle frequently uses religious symbolism in her works. In *The Arm of the Starfish* Gaea is described as a paradise, and the main character Adam is tempted by the beautiful Kali. Joshua, who can be considered a Christ figure, does not appear in L'Engle's initial outline of the manuscript but plays a major role in the story. How does the use of Joshua as an integral character change the story?

_____

_____

_____

_____

_____

_____

Writing About Madeleine L'Engle's *The Arm of the Starfish*

Focusing on Plot

L'Engle bases the plot of *The Arm of the Starfish* on the regenerative abilities of the starfish. When a starfish loses an arm, it has the ability to grow it back again. One helpful guideline for science fiction writers is to base their work on a believable rule or scientific principle and then to ask "what if?" L'Engle does just that when she asks, "What if the same properties of regeneration in the starfish could be used for humans?" What are the rules that L'Engle sets up and follows throughout the story? Discuss those rules in small groups and list them below.

_____

_____

How do the rules apply to Macrina and Temis? How do they apply to the starfish, frogs, and lizards in which Dr. O'Keefe's corrupt lab assistant transposed nerve rings?

_____

_____

Discuss with group members the ethics of Dr. O'Keefe's experiments and similar genetic experiments. List the ideas of your group members on another sheet of paper.

Focusing on Good Versus Evil

Kali arranges to meet Adam at the airport before he leaves the United States. There she warns him of evil things and tells him to beware of Canon Tallis and Dr. Calvin O'Keefe. Kali's beauty influences Adam and makes her seem good. However, he quickly becomes quite confused as to which side is good and which side is evil. He learns that in life it is often difficult to distinguish between the two. In Chapter 9 Adam wishes that the difference between the good and the evil sides would become black and white. Then he remembers the time when his math teacher told about his first encounter with higher level math problems and his confusion because they did not have one simple answer. In your small group look through the book to find evidence of good and evil on both sides.

On another sheet of paper, write about the difficulty Adam has in deciding with which side to align his service and loyalty. How does Kali serve to confuse him even further?

WHOEVER HEARD
OF A
TALKING
HORSE !!

Name _____

Writing With Madeleine L'Engle

Embedding Science Fiction in Reality

Science fiction writers often begin with a scientific rule or principle and then use their imaginations to visualize something a bit out of the ordinary. One way to achieve this extraordinary state is to ask, "What if?" Either with a partner or alone, ask yourself the following "what if" questions. Put your answers on another sheet of paper.

What if
humans could travel into the past—or the future?

humans could change in size?

we could stop (or reverse) the aging process?

humans could become invisible at will?

colors did not exist?

everyone were equal in every way?

the intelligence levels of humans could be changed?

humans could control the weather?

humans could live under water, in space, or underground?

there were no _____ (diseases, books, words)?

animals could talk?

humans could read other people's minds?

time ran backwards?

there was no school?

Select one of the above, or create a "what if?" situation of your own, and write two possible plot outlines based on that situation. What scientific principle will you need to know or to study in order to write a believable story?

Putting It All Together

Using your study of science fiction, *The Arm of the Starfish,* your "Embedding Science Fiction in Reality" activity (page 125), and your study of the appropriate scientific concepts, write the first draft of a science fiction story. Be certain to include the following elements.

Researching Scientific Principles. Create a list of scientific principles upon which you plan to base your story. Read about those topics in science books, encyclopedias, and science periodicals. Take accurate notes.

Establishing the Setting. If your story involves travel of any kind, you will need to include more than one setting. Remember L'Engle's description of the fog at Kennedy International Airport, the winding streets and sites of Lisbon, and the serenity of Gaea. Try to use all of your senses when establishing the setting(s) for your story.

Developing Characters. Like L'Engle you may want to revive a character from an earlier work by looking through your previous writing. If you do reuse a character, be certain that your physical description of the character is true to the first work and have the character age appropriately from story to story. Create (or reuse) one or more characters to be on the "good" side and one or more characters to be on the "evil" side.

Plotting the Action. Using the ideas from the "Embedding Science Fiction in Reality" activity (page 125), outline the main events that will take place in the story. Remember that Joshua did not even appear in L'Engle's outline for the manuscript. Like L'Engle, you may add or delete events, characters, and settings as you draft your story.

Adding Details. L'Engle borrowed lines from a Robert Frost poem and used them as a pass code. Several of her characters could speak different languages. And Dr. O'Keefe double coded his reports. You may wish to include similar details in your story to add suspense.

When you are finished with your first draft, read it to several other members of your class. Ask them for suggestions.

Write your final draft.

Compile all finished stories in a classroom science fiction anthology titled "Science Fiction Thrillers" or as a group create a title of your own.